T0013195

The
BUSHCRAFT
FIELD GUIDE TO
TRAPPING,
GATHERING,
&COOKING
IN THE WILD

DAVE CANTERBURY
New York Times Bestselling Author of *Bushcraft 101*

Adams Media
New York London Toronto Sydney New Delhi

Adams Media
An Imprint of Simon & Schuster, Inc.
100 Technology Center Drive
Stoughton, MA 02072

For information about special discounts for bulk purchases, please contact Simon & Schuster Special Sales at 1-866-506-1949 or business@simonandschuster.com.

The Simon & Schuster Speakers Bureau can bring authors to your live event. For more information or to book an event contact the Simon & Schuster Speakers Bureau at 1-866-248-3049 or visit our website at www.simonspeakers.com.

Interior illustrations by Eric Andrews.

Insert photos © iStockphoto.com and 123RF.

Manufactured in the United States of America

18 2022

Library of Congress Cataloging-in-Publication Data has been applied for.

ISBN 978-1-4405-9852-4
ISBN 978-1-4405-9853-1 (ebook)

Many of the designations used by manufacturers and sellers to distinguish their products are claimed as trademarks. Where those designations appear in this book and Simon & Schuster, Inc., was aware of a trademark claim, the designations have been printed with initial capital letters.

Readers are urged to take all appropriate precautions before undertaking any how-to task. Always read and follow instructions and safety warnings for all tools and materials, and call in a professional if the task stretches your abilities too far. Although every effort has been made to provide the best possible information in this book, neither the publisher nor the author are responsible for accidents, injuries, or damage incurred as a result of tasks undertaken by readers. This book is not a substitute for professional services.

DEDICATION

I would like to dedicate this book to my loving granddaughter Layla. In the many books, articles, and other forms of media I generate, I wish that she will be able to see me and read my words many years from now and that her children may know who their grandfather was, and that he enjoyed passing on the knowledge of his forefathers so that she may pass on this knowledge to future generations through my written words. I think that leaving a legacy for others to enjoy is a true blessing and gift from God, and this gift I dedicate to her.

Acknowledgments

When you begin to research for a book or you begin to study a subject in depth you inevitably look for sources of information you can trust to learn from, then you go out and you practice what you have read or seen, and you quickly get a feel for what actually works for you. In cooking, everyone has a different taste for what they like and you adapt to make the foods taste good to you.

So when I began to look through source materials I found myself going right back to some of the great authors I had learned from in the past as they had already adapted many methods of cooking to the wilderness. The great thing about the outdoors is eating in it! Nothing tastes quite as good as it does when cooked over an open fire.

To that end authors like Horace Kephart, George Washington Sears, Hyatt Verrill, Steven Watts, David Wescott, Ellsworth Jaeger, Bernard Mason, Warren Miller, and many others already have valuable information on what apparatus to use for cooking this or that, and how to adapt that kitchen recipe to the field. All one has to do is practice it and adapt it to his personal gear selection and taste for foods. So to that end I have compiled this book on camp cooking according to my style of woodland cooking. I thank all of the above authors and many others for their tireless efforts to educate us all in the skills that have somewhat become lost in modern times. And with this book I hope to rekindle that love of cooking in the great outdoors.

I would last but not least say that truly God is the provider and we benefit from the vast amount of resources he has provided. It is our responsibility to understand how to utilize them so that we can become more self-reliant.

Contents

CHAPTER 10: TYPES OF COOKING   119

PART 3: LIVING OFF THE LAND   127

CHAPTER 11: HUNTING AND TRAPPING GAME: FUNDAMENTALS   129

CHAPTER 12: HUNTING: BEYOND THE BASICS   137

— Introduction —

This book will be useful to anyone who recreates outdoors whether it be for a day hike, a trail hike, a weekend camp, or a longer-term hunting trek. It is written with the ultimate goal of understanding the difference between wants and needs when it comes to foods and their preparations.

When we think about bushcraft, especially when we introduce survival mentality into the equation, we often think of living completely off the land and meeting all of our food intake needs from the resources around us within the landscape. However, the fact is we will spend much more time in nature on a recreational basis than in a true survival situation.

At the same time we cannot go on a weeklong hunting camp and expect to live completely from what we can provide by rod and gun or even necessarily from traps and foraging. Seasonality plays a large role in foraging. Weather can affect game movements, and we are at the mercy of the season for legal take. Size limits restrict fishing . . . the list goes on. So we cannot expect in the modern day to just wander off with a few friends and live completely off the land even for a week in most areas and in most seasons.

To that end many books have been written over the years that speak to what implements and foods we can take with us and how best to store and use it, what implements we will need for food preparation, and what different food offerings can be made from just a few simple sundries.

Sometimes we can take more extravagant amounts of cooking kit and foodstuffs with us depending on our form of conveyance, and other times we are limited to what we can personally carry. Understanding this and adapting can make life on the trail very comfortable and allow us to "smooth it" as the sportswriter and conservationist Nessmuk would say.

This book is an attempt to capture the gear, methods, and types of sundries we have available to us now to get food from our surroundings. While I'll include traditional foods and methods of gathering, catching, and preparing food, I'll also give attention to what we have available now that may not have been attainable for those writing in the past.

It is no secret that there is romance in living as close to nature as possible. Roasting a nice piece of fresh game meat over the fire on a forked stick, while a small ash cake is cooking within the coals, and a nice cup of hot coffee poured from the kettle sets the tone for an evening of true woodsmanship under the stars. We should take advantage of this at every opportunity, but we should also be prepared to use what we can pack to supplement that food if things don't work out as we had hoped.

While we can fashion cooking implements from natural materials to help us cut weight from packing them in, we should also realize many items available in the modern day make cooking very convenient. New materials like titanium weigh less for an entire cook kit than a single pan carried in the 1920s and 1930s. We must understand what types of materials suit our needs best and know the pros and cons of these materials, as well as what implements we can fashion from the woods to aid us in cooking, especially if we are packing in by foot and cannot afford the weight of heavy fire irons and such.

In the same respect if we are to be well-rounded and educated woodsmen, we must also be able to create many items needed for preparing our food off the landscape. This knowledge will make an emergency situation a bit less hectic. Were we to lose our kit from, say, a canoe rolling with our pack in it, washing our beloved cook set down river, we still need to make it back to our home and family, and we may need to walk a day or more to get there. We will need to know how to acquire food, disinfect water, and possibly cook without many tools on hand.

Even if we don't have an emergency, being able to hunt, trap, fish, and forage allows us to supplement the foodstuffs we have, making more variety in our meals as well as extending our provisions. Understanding the nutritional value of plants and animals and knowing how to cook them will make us not only more at home in the natural world but more self-reliant and allow us to rely less on carried items and foodstuffs in the long run.

In survival, food is nowhere near the top of the list of priorities to stay alive especially in the short term. But I will say that variety within the diet and good food makes a lot of misfortune much easier to swallow.

Within this book we will explore everything from what types of foods we should carry for a balanced diet on the trail to what we can forage from the natural world to supplement that food, as well as what implements we should carry depending on our aim, and what we can manufacture even as it may pertain to an emergency.

We will look at how to best save room within our outfit by carrying easy-to-prepare foods as well as how to process wild foods we have harvested from the landscape. We will talk about gathering meat sources from a perspective of additional foods but these methods could also apply in an emergency if we carry the knowledge to manufacture needed items as well.

—*Dave Canterbury*

PART 1
Packed-In Food

— Chapter 1 —
DECIDING
WHAT TO BRING

"Variety is as welcome at the camp board as anywhere else. In fact more so for it is harder to get."

—HORACE KEPHART

Understanding what to pack should be the first priority when venturing out, just as much as leaving a good game plan with someone close to you in case of an emergency. I tell my students there are really five key items that need to be within any pack at the onset of a trip:

- Cutting tool
- Combustion or fire-making devices
- Cover, including clothing that will protect you from the elements
- Metal container that can be placed into a fire if needed
- Cordage for use in bindings and lashings

These simple items will help protect the most important thing, which is your body's core temperature. Hypothermia (getting too cold) and heat exhaustion (getting too hot) are the main killers in outdoor emergencies. These five items are all used to manipulate the surroundings to control the body's core temperature.

These five items are also the most difficult to reproduce from the landscape, requiring specific materials, skill sets, and sometimes great amounts of time.

CUTTING TOOL

The knife must be capable of many things, from cutting small limbs from trees to butchering game. You should always have a backup, like a pocket knife, as well. But your primary blade should be a sheath knife that you keep on your hip. Secure it well so it will never be lost. It should have a 5" blade in case it is needed when other tools are not present to process fire materials, be a full tang (one solid piece with the handle attached) so that it is strong enough to stand abuse, have a sharp 90° edge on the spine to aid in tinder processing or scraping a ferrocerium rod, and be made of high-carbon steel for use as a last-emergency fire resource for flint-and-steel ignition.

COMBUSTION AND FIRE-MAKING DEVICES

The combustion device you choose is a matter of personal preference. For me, I want three such devices, all in my pockets with backups in the pack:

1. A Bic lighter is about the most foolproof device ever made for creating flame. If conserved and used properly it will give you fire in almost any weather.

2. A ferrocerium rod (ferro rod), which can be purchased for a few dollars at a sporting goods store, can come in handy and help conserve the lighter if tinder sources are prime or highly combustible.
3. A magnification lens can be used as a renewable resource, especially if used in conjunction with making char (which is always a priority as it helps all three devices last much longer).

COVER

For clothing, pack at least two full sets of socks and undergarments, trousers, and shirts. Carry clothing that is comfortable in all seasons. Do not forget to plan for rain and wet weather. In winter, use a heavy wool layer that will act as insulation. Nothing beats wool in cold-weather climates. If freezing rain and sleet are an issue, combine the wool with an oilcloth raincoat.

Leather boots are an absolute must for long-term wilderness activities. Remember that boots are only as waterproof as they are high. Carrying a second pair of boots will save a lot of trouble on long trips so you can alternate and avoid wearing them out. If carrying a second pair is too cumbersome, bring a pair of moccasins to wear when walking around camp so that you give your boots an occasional rest.

A good hat will protect you from the sun and conserve body heat—most of which is released through the head and the neck. Kerchiefs and scarves have been staples of the woodsman's kit for hundreds of years and have many versatile uses.

A sturdy pair of leather calfskin gloves will protect the hands from briars, brambles, and blisters when doing normal camp chores. In winter, arctic mittens with wool glove liners are indispensable.

In addition, you'll need a cover element for normal environmental changes. It should be large enough to cover an area as long as you are tall plus 2' and have good, sturdy tie-out points for suspension if needed. This should be combined with an emergency space blanket (the heavy, reusable kind) and an emergency bivvy (heat-reflecting blanket). These are very lightweight and the size of a softball when compressed.

Small backpacking-style tents provide comfort and security from bugs and other wigglers. The downside is that their construction restricts your view and eliminates the ability to use fire as a heat source. There is always a tradeoff with any piece of gear. There are a lot of different types of tents on the market, but I would suggest selecting one that is made of the heaviest material you feel comfortable carrying. You will appreciate the durability.

METAL CONTAINER

A metal container can be aluminum, stainless, or titanium, but stainless is the strongest and most durable. It should have a nesting cup of the same material that can stand the full flames of a fire.

CORDAGE

Your cordage should be multiple-ply so that it can be broken down to small enough fibers for sewing if needed, but strong enough to hold a ridge beam as well. A #36 tarred bank line is what I recommend.

Beyond these five essentials, I find five more simple items to be of the most use. These will also make an emergency first-aid kit when combined with the others:

- Large cotton bandanna or cloth at least 36" × 36"
- Roll of duct tape
- Headlamp

- Compass with a mirror and movable bezel ring
- Sail-maker's needle

This entire kit should weigh less than 10 pounds, and from this we build our basic kit for woods running.

Now to the pack itself. The size of the pack is dictated by what we carry or the conveyance available to us. Assuming you are carrying the pack at least part of the time, you won't want anything too large, but a pack that's too small won't carry what you need.

A day pack is too small and an expedition pack too big, so stay with something in the 35–70 liter range, depending on your body size. Other factors to consider are the amount of time you are planning to be out. Is it only a night or is it two or three? Some of the added weight can be counteracted by using foodstuffs that can make multiple different foods with a few additions, like instant biscuits or dried beans and rice. You must also consider your own fitness level when carrying any load. The maximum load most find to be comfortable walking over distance is about 30–35 pounds. If you are trekking any more than a day or two you should allow at least 10 pounds of this weight for food, cook gear, and water.

There are hundreds of pack brands on the market to choose from in many styles and colors.

Choose a pack that has been made from a durable material such as heavy nylon or canvas. Either of these makes a good choice in materials as they can take much abuse. A military surplus pack that has good solid buckles and straps is purpose-built to take the rigors of the outdoors and is a good low-cost choice to start with.

Remember that the larger the pack the more we are tempted to pack, and the more pockets and pouches we have the harder it is to find what we need. I like a single-bucket design with maybe one outer pocket or flap pocket myself. A waist belt on a pack as well as a chest strap will make it much more manageable under load over distance for sure and this should be considered if that is the intended use of the pack itself.

If the pack is simply a storage facility to be placed into conveyance I would suggest heavy material and straps so that it is durable enough to withstand being jostled and thrown in and out of a boat or sled, or on and off horses or ATVs.

NUTRITIONAL NEEDS

When you're choosing what food to pack in on your trip, you'll need to weigh a number of considerations, including how long you'll be gone, how much food you can reasonably expect to gather or catch from the land, and how you'll be carrying your equipment and gear—whether you'll be trekking by foot or using vehicles for transportation.

Our first consideration is nutrition. The body needs certain inputs to operate and function at optimal levels. Among these are protein, carbohydrates, fats, minerals, and vitamins. But the most important is water. Most people need about 4 quarts of water per day. Exercise increases that amount up to and sometimes more than 6 quarts. One of your first decisions is how to make sure you have enough water.

PROTEIN

In the daily diet, proteins are provided through many sources that include lean meat and nuts as well as dairy products. Supplemental protein powders also contain large volumes of proteins and these are generally mixed with water or milk, making them easier for the body to metabolize. Look at any trail energy bar and the main listing on the front of the package will be grams of protein.

Many of the protein powders on the market will last a long time. Some come in large plastic containers that can be used for other things after. Find one that is at least 30 or 40 grams of protein per serving and that mixes well with water. Country Cream is a good brand that actually tastes like milk when mixed with water. This can add daily protein and vitamins when used as recipe ingredients or just consumed as a liquid. Ovaltine and similar mixes will also increase vitamin and mineral intake.

Energy bars are a good choice as well, but the commercial breakfast bars are more palatable in most cases and full of good nutrition as well.

CARBOHYDRATES AND FATS

Carbohydrates and fats will give you needed daily energy for exercise, to fuel your body, and to help generate heat. You can get much of this from simple sugars, found in many candies and sweets, but you also need more complex sugars produced from carbohydrates that come from starchy foods such as potatoes, breads, and pastas. So-called "whole grains" provide your body with necessary nutrients like iron and folic acid, along with fiber, which helps your digestion.

You need both carbohydrates and fats for energy. Your body uses calories from carbohydrates first, but then after about 20 minutes of effort, your body begins burning calories from fat. Fat has other benefits as well: It helps your body process fat-soluble vitamins such as A, D, E, and K; it helps insulate your body; and it produces fatty acids that your body needs for brain development, blood clotting, and other bodily functions.

VITAMINS AND MINERALS

Vitamins are organic compounds that your body needs for normal cell growth and function.

Types of Vitamins

There are two types of vitamins, those that are fat-soluble and those that are water-soluble:

- **Fat-soluble vitamins** are those that bind to fat in the stomach and are then stored in the body for later use. We are less likely to become deficient in these vitamins (A, D, E, and K), but more likely to build up toxic levels of them, usually due to extreme overconsumption or overzealous supplement use. (Or maybe just an unhealthy obsession with kale chips . . .)
- **Water-soluble vitamins** make up the rest of the 13 essential vitamins. They can be absorbed directly by cells. When in excess, these vitamins are flushed out of our system with each bathroom break. The water-soluble vitamins—vitamin C and the B complex vitamins, including biotin, niacin, folic acid, and pantothenic acid—need to be restored more frequently, but the body can tolerate higher doses.

Minerals

Minerals are inorganic substances (meaning they contain no carbon) that your body needs to function, and all hold a place on the good ol' Periodic Table (flashback to sixth-grade chemistry class!). There are two groups of minerals: macrominerals like calcium and sodium, which the body needs in large doses, and trace minerals, like selenium and chromium (only a pinch required).

While very important in the long term, vitamins and minerals are less of a major concern short term. However, while in camp it never hurts to stock up on the immune-boosting qualities of vitamins like vitamin C. Some forms of drink mixes provide a heavy dose of immune system boosters. Certain pine needle teas and other plant teas have very high amounts of this vitamin as well. Depending on your experience level and comfort level in the woods, stress and lack of sleep can play great detriment to the overall immune system and it is much easier to get rundown and sick in these situations.

PINE NEEDLE TEA

Pine needle tea is high in vitamin C. Be careful on species selection as there are pines that are toxic if consumed. For example, you will want to avoid ponderosa pines, Norfolk Island pines (also called Australian pines), and yew trees (the yew is not a pine tree but is sometimes mistaken for one). Lodge-pole and Monterey pines may give you digestive troubles.

To make a simple pine needle tea, bring water to a rolling boil and remove from fire. Add a handful of green needles. Chopped is best to release the volatile oils. Place a lid over the container and let steep about 15 minutes, then strain and consume. There is no set ratio of the number of needles to water. Just experiment to find what suits your taste.

DAILY CALORIES

The amount of calories needed daily to maintain good health and the breakdown of these calories depends on age, weight, and other physical conditions, such as how much you exercise. It is generally based on what's called the BMI, or body mass index. There are online calculators that will give you the breakdown of what your daily caloric intake needs should be and how those calories should be supplied.

However, for this discussion we can look at an average for a healthy active male and see that 2,000–3,000 calories per day is a suggested amount of food intake (for women it is 1,800–2,500 calories). Approximately 45–65 percent of total calories should come from carbohydrates, 20–35 percent from fat, and 10–35 percent from protein.

What these numbers really stand for is what you should strive for on a daily basis to maintain good health. However, when we are camped and relaxing or on a hunting trip these concerns of perfection in portioning don't mean a whole lot. It is better for us to understand that a good variety and a balanced meal will make any trip more enjoyable for all and if the side benefits are great food and enough energy to get our daily activities accomplished, well, then that is what we were after.

See Appendix A for the nutritional values of various game animals and of various nuts.

WATER

As stated previously, water is one of the most important daily requirements for good health. From a camp standpoint, water provides needed liquid for coffee, tea, hot chocolate, and mixing with "Just Add Water" (JAW) foods.

The problem is we don't want to carry a lot of it because it's heavy. One gallon of water weighs 8 pounds.

Now, we know that we should always camp near a water source if possible. This is one of the 4 Ws of selecting a good camp location (Wood, Water, Wind, and Widowmakers are discussed in my book *Bushcraft 101*).

However, after selecting the site you must be able to make that groundwater resource potable. Most things you would cook that use water will need that water to be hot anyway so boiling is the easiest and safest method to create potable water in the short term. Filtering that water before boiling will make it even better.

Water disinfection tablets like chlorine dioxide and iodine tabs are very useful tools. But it must be understood that chlorine dioxide tabs are actually poison in large amounts, and iodine can have adverse effects on health in certain circumstances as well. In addition, they cannot kill giardia, a type of parasite that causes stomach distress. However, with all that said they are very good to have as an emergency backup to boiling. Use them in conjunction with filtration if chemical contamination is a concern.

BUSHCRAFT TIP

Keep these four elements in mind when making camp:

1. **Water:** Always camp near a water source because traveling a long distance daily for this can become an issue especially if an injury is sustained during the camp or if no large containers are available to hold water.

2. **Wood:** You will want plenty of this precious resource nearby, not only for cooking but for warmth.

3. **Wind:** The wind direction can be important from a smoke standpoint. Smoke from your fire should be blown away from your shelter, not driven toward it. It is always best to set a fire lay with crosswind to help feed the fire. Also, wind direction indicates weather. If you do not want rain blowing in on you with an open shelter you must pay attention when building it.

4. **Widowmakers:** These are dead standing trees in the proximity of your camp and nearby that could fall during a wind or storm, causing equipment damage or personal injury.

FILTERING WATER

There are many apparatus on the market today that will do a pretty good job and most products name a percentage of contaminants they will remove on the package. However, I go back to the cooking and say if we can cook, we can boil!

If you want to filter the water before boiling to remove turbidity or sediments or just to give yourself better peace of mind that it is as clean as you can get it on the fly or in a temporary camp, there are a couple of ways to create filters.

You can also carry some type of pump filter to remove most contaminants prior to boiling.

You can build a makeshift filter. This is not difficult given the proper materials at hand. Make a tripod from 3 saplings about 2" in diameter and 6' long. Use 3 tiers of a fabric like a bandanna tied to the tripod to create nests that material can be placed into. The first layer should receive some course filtering media like grass or weeds, the second should be charcoal from the fire if possible (not ash), and the final tier should be sand.

Pour water slowly from the top and let drain through the tiers into a catch basin. Then boil the water that is in the catch basin. It may take a couple runs through the filter to get clean-appearing water. This will help filter large particulates from the water but will not replace a good ceramic-type filter if available—a makeshift filter is an emergency measure. See Figure 1.1.

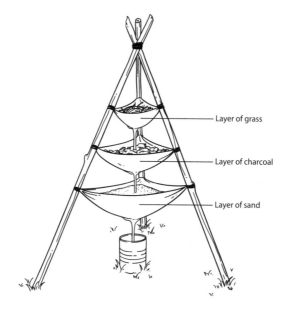

Layer of grass

Layer of charcoal

Layer of sand

Figure 1.1 Tripod water filter

Another method is to use a 2-liter bottle top as a funnel, inverting it and placing it in the bottom portion of the bottle. You layer the same filter mediums inside. See Figure 1.2.

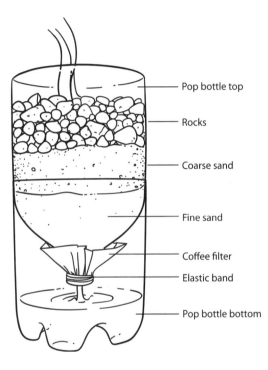

Pop bottle top

Rocks

Coarse sand

Fine sand

Coffee filter

Elastic band

Pop bottle bottom

Figure 1.2 Funnel water filter

BOILING WATER

To make water potable by boiling, bring it to a boil at 212°F (100°C). Letting it boil for 10 minutes will eliminate most of the bugs that cause intestinal distress. However, boiling doesn't remove chemical toxins, which is one reason you may also want to use filtering.

If you're boiling hard water—water with a lot of calcium salts dissolved in it—you'll find that a deposit will build up on your utensils. This can be removed with vinegar.

Boiling does not permanently eliminate microbes from the water. If the boiled water is stored, microbes can collect. So you only need to boil as much water as you are likely to use up in the near future.

TIPS AND TRICKS

- For clothing, I recommend 10- to 12-ounce durable canvas pants like the tree-climbing pants offered by Arborwear. Long-sleeved, lightweight, canvas, button-down shirts are comfortable in all seasons, and cotton T-shirts take advantage of evaporative cooling in the summer.
- Moccasins, elk hide or buffalo, are handy when stalking game in dry leaves.
- Look for varieties of tents with mesh tops and a rain flap, which helps alleviate condensation issues.
- I prefer to carry packets of Emergen-C for daily use as an immune booster.
- Ceramic-type filters from companies like LifeStraw, Sawyer, and Aquamira are almost 100 percent effective for disinfecting groundwater resources.

— Chapter 2 —
FOODS THAT REQUIRE MINIMAL PROCESSING

"A crude meal, no doubt, but the best of all sauces is hunger."
—EDWARD ABBEY, *DESERT SOLITAIRE*

Many of the foods today that we can carry require very little to no processing before consumption. You don't have to cook an apple in order to eat it—but the tradeoff is that apples can be heavy to carry. Lighter in weight and easier to carry are more processed foods like energy bars and similar types of food, but none that I have tasted make a meal that is fit for the woods. So consider carrying in food that requires a little preparation but which will provide a more satisfying meal to accompany your outdoor adventure.

TRAIL MIXES AND SNACKS

Trail mixes combine most of the needed food nutrients we want, and these are great snacks, although again not much of a meal for the woodsy traveler. Good trail mix contains a high-protein nut like a cashew or almond, some type of dried fruit like a raisin for concentrated nutrition, and chocolate for quick energy. You can make similar mixes at home.

Trail snacks, like pemmican and fruit leathers, can also be a good way to tame hunger pangs when you don't have time to stop and build a fire.

DAVE'S HOMEMADE TRAIL MIX

This is about 3 days' food if needed in an emergency.

1 cup dried bananas
1 cup raisins
1 cup Hershey's chocolate morsels
2 cups cashew halves
1 cup pecans
1 cup walnuts

Mix well and store in a 32-ounce water bottle for carry.

SIMPLE TRAIL MIX

A simple, less expensive trail mix.

8 ounces raisins
8 ounces mixed nuts (or peanuts, an even cheaper option)
8 ounces sunflower seeds
8 ounces chocolate chips
Salt, to taste

Mix together all ingredients. Add salt to taste. Enjoy!

SIMPLE PEMMICAN

You can make this pemmican ahead of time or at camp.
If making it at camp, do everything except melting the lard well away
from the fire so that the pemmican can solidify.

8 ounces beef jerky, finely minced
1 cup fresh raspberries
½ cup lard

Mash jerky and raspberries together in a bowl to form a paste-like mixture.

Melt lard. Stir jerky-raspberry mixture into pot, away from heat.

Pour into a sheet of cotton cloth (about 12" × 12") and twist into a ball. Let stand in a cool area to dry.

Once solidified this can be carried for days and eaten on the trail as needed.

FRUIT LEATHER

In a pinch, the leather can be dried on the dashboard inside a car.

1½ cups fresh raspberries
1 teaspoon honey

Purée the raspberries. You can use an egg beater, food processor, or mortar and pestle for this.

Add honey to raspberries and mix well.

Place a plastic sheet or polytarp section on a table. Spread the purée mixture in a thin layer onto the plastic. It should be about ⅛" thick. Leave in full sun to dry (be sure to keep insects away).

The leather is done when it is dry and can be peeled up in a sheet from the plastic. This usually takes 6–8 hours. If it is not done in a single day's heat, you can store, covered, in a cool place and repeat the next day.

PRECOOKED OR PRE-PREPPED FOODS

It does not take much of a fire to heat a kettle. Many foods are easily prepared within their packages now by just warming them. The biggest advantages to precooked or pre-prepped foods are the time they save and the packaging they come in, which prevents spoilage at ambient temperature. Many of these foods come in a single-serving bag or can serve 2 people. They also make great additives to other foods in larger recipes.

BAGGED FOODS

Many types of dried or easy-to-prepare foods come in bags and may be worth consideration. Good examples of foods that come in bags and are not packed in much liquid, saving space, weight, and room, are:

- Uncle Ben's Rice
- StarKist Tuna
- Hormel Bacon
- Santa Fe Refried Beans

These are some of my favorite meals to make with bagged foods, like rice:

JERKY AND RICE BUSH POT

I like using Uncle Ben's Ready Rice for this as it is an easy, quick trail meal.

1 package precooked rice (8–9 ounces)
4 ounces beef jerky

Heat rice for several minutes in a pot of boiling water (leave in bag). Remove from heat. Cut open bag and add beef jerky, then close bag and let stand in the pot of hot water for about 20 minutes. Season to taste.

TEX-MEX BUSH POT

*This meal can stand alone or be served
with a tortilla and grated Cheddar cheese.*

1 package precooked southwestern rice (8–9 ounces)
1½ cups water
6-ounce can of precooked ground beef
1 teaspoon chili powder

Add rice to pot with water. Boil until the mix is heated and thickens. Add beef and chili powder. Cook until heated through. Serve.

CHICKEN CASSEROLE

You can use leftover chicken for this recipe instead of precooked.

1 package precooked wild rice (8–9 ounces)
1½ cups water
1 package precooked chicken (about 12 ounces)
2 tablespoons dehydrated vegetables
¼ teaspoon garlic
¼ teaspoon Old Bay Seasoning
Parmesan cheese, grated

Add all ingredients except cheese to pot. Cook down until thick on low heat. Top with Parmesan cheese and serve with bread or biscuits if desired.

CURRY CHICKEN AND RICE

*I like Uncle Ben's Butter & Garlic Ready Rice for this dish,
but you can use your preference.*

1 package precooked chicken (about 12 ounces)
1 package precooked rice (8–9 ounces)
1½ cups water
Curry powder, to taste

Add all ingredients to pot and cook over low heat until rice is cooked and chicken is heated through. Serve with bread.

CANNED FOODS

Canned foods are another example in the quick-and-easy category, but care must be taken to check just how much liquid is used in the canning of the product or you may be wasting weight carrying water and could easily substitute something else of less weight and bulk.

Now with that said, from where I stand there is one great advantage to canned food: You have a ready container after the fact for drinking or for cooking other food later without carrying a separate pot. This can be especially handy on a short trip.

The best types of canned foods have pull-top lids so there are no jagged edges from the opening process.

Foods in this category that are readily available are:

- Yoders canned meats
- Hormel Chili
- Campbell's stews
- Van Camp's Pork and Beans

JARRED FOODS

Some foods that come in plastic jars don't require refrigeration after opening and are worth a mention if for no other reason than emergencies. These foods include peanut butter and honey. Alone and without some type of bread or crackers, this is a rough lunch indeed, but it can become a welcome gift in an emergency. Peanut butter and honey are the perfect short-term survival foods in my mind. You will also find jams, jellies, and sauces come in jars and can add a special touch to a meal.

Unfortunately glass jars require special care to keep from breaking. They can be wrapped in things like a layer of bubble wrap or heavy cloth and then duct-taped for travel if needed. Most foods found in glass jars these days can be found in or transferred to plastic jars if needed.

DEHYDRATED FOODS

There are also lots of foods on the market that are dehydrated and only require that water be added to make them very palatable and in most cases very tasty. I am not referring in this text to dehydrated camp meals in a bag, as I find the majority very bland indeed but instead mean inexpensive foods that can be added to other ingredients to make a meal. Again many of these type foods need only be added in some quantity to other bagged foods like rice or beans to make an excellent meal.

There are two types of dehydrated foods, those that require the addition of hot water and those that just require the addition of water.

JAHW (JUST ADD HOT WATER)

If you're going to be lighting a fire for cooking or warmth anyway, dehydrated foods that require hot water are simple to use and can add a lot of variety to your meals.

Soup greens by Harmony House are a good example. They can be purchased in bulk from many places and are a staple in my outdoor pantry. They add flavor to any meal as well as providing needed vitamins and nutrients.

HUNTER'S STIR-FRY

This is a great recipe that uses dehydrated soup greens.

2 tablespoons olive oil
2 tablespoons dehydrated soup greens, rehydrated
1 cup (or the amount to your liking) fresh game meat, diced
Seasoned salt, to taste

Add oil to skillet placed over a medium-hot part of the fire. Add greens and meat. Cook through, stirring occasionally. Add seasoned salt to taste, then serve.

Dehydrated potatoes are another great example of this. There are several brands as well as flavors out there. These can also be used to thicken a stew made in the pot; add while simmering.

RICE AND SAUSAGE DINNER

You can use any kind of pork or game sausage for this dish.

½ pound sausage
1 package Knorr Rice Sides (about 5–6 ounces), flavor of choice
2 cups water
2 tablespoons instant potatoes

Brown sausage in skillet over medium flame. Add rice and water. Bring to a boil. Remove to a less hot part of the fire and let simmer. Add potatoes to thicken a few minutes before serving. Serve over fresh toasted bread.

QUICK CHICKEN AND DUMPLINGS

1 package precooked chicken (about 12 ounces)
1 chicken-flavored bouillon cube
½ of a 4-ounce package (about ¼ cup) instant potatoes
1 teaspoon dehydrated vegetables
¼ teaspoon Old Bay Seasoning
1 package just-add-water biscuit mix (about 7 ounces)

Add all ingredients except biscuit mix to bush pot. Fill about ¾ full with water. Bring contents to a boil and let reduce to ½.

While stew is boiling, prepare biscuit mix according to package directions. Drop 1" lumps into boiling liquid. Dumplings will form. Add a few at a time to a total of about 4–5.

When dumplings are cooked through (about 3–4 minutes), serve stew.

SAUSAGE GRAVY

1 pound sausage (can be any sausage of game meat or pork)
1 packet (about 1 ounce) peppered gravy mix
1 cup cold water (or amount indicated on gravy mix packet)

Fry meat in pan on medium heat until browned. Add gravy mix and water. Stir on a lower heat until thick and sausage is cooked through. Serve on any breakfast bread or biscuit.

JAW (JUST ADD WATER)

Many types of mixes for breads, cakes, cookies, pancakes, biscuits, and muffins are on the market now that only require the addition of water to make an excellent addition to or dessert for any camp meal. So many batter-type mixes are available now that it almost makes carrying the old standards of flour, baking soda, and baking powder obsolete. The usefulness of the JAHW and JAW foods is only as limited as the imagination.

There are a great many brands of these items on the market today. Sometimes the best places to find them are at discount and dollar stores. Look for mixes that specifically say "complete" or "just add water." Biscuit-type mixes are very versatile and can be used for everything from drop biscuits to ash cakes to hush puppies to dumplings. They can be used as stew thickeners as well.

CORN FRY BREAD

This is a simple fry bread recipe using a just-add-water mix.

1 package (about 6½ ounces) just-add-water corn bread mix
Water as per mix instructions
1 tablespoon granulated sugar
Bacon grease or lard for frying

Stir together corn bread mix, water, and sugar. This should form a mixture thick enough to form cakes by hand. Fry in skillet with bacon grease or lard over medium heat, until browned on both sides.

HUSH PUPPIES AND CREAM CHEESE

You may be used to eating your hush puppies with mayonnaise or ketchup (or nothing at all), but give cream cheese a try!

1 package just-add-water hush puppy mix
Water as per mix instructions
Vegetable oil for deep-frying
Cream cheese spread

Mix instant hush puppy mix in a bag with water to form a thick batter that will fall from a spoon in a lump. Heat 2–3" of oil in a skillet.

Once oil is heated, drop balls of mix into hot oil. They should rise almost immediately to the top. Turn once during cooking. Cook about 2–3 minutes each side. Remove when brown. Serve with cream cheese spread.

TIPS AND TRICKS

- Mother Earth Products sells single vegetables in bulk dehydrated as well as fruits and other mixes for soups.
- You can repackage some items at home to reduce bulk and weight (throw out the box but keep the inner envelope, for example).
- One key safety element when reusing cans is to ensure, if you plan to drink from this container, that you check for sharp edges.
- The nutritional value of peanut butter alone makes it well worth having a small jar in any kit.
- Pancake-type mixes are much less versatile than other mixes but can be used for some things.
- Dried milk is a great asset if you choose a good brand. Country Cream is a good one for sure.
- Powdered eggs can replace fresh ones in anything needing them including just straight-up scrambled eggs or omelets. I recommend Sonstegard brand.

Chapter 3

WHOLE FOODS
THAT DON'T REQUIRE
REFRIGERATION

"After a good dinner one can forgive anybody, even one's own relations."

—Oscar Wilde

When deciding what foods to pack in, you want to avoid items that need to be kept cool or refrigerated. It is difficult to maintain a specific environment for your food so it's a good idea to choose products that can tolerate tough conditions.

Many of these foods require cooking, but their preparation doesn't have to be complicated or time-consuming. You'll find a variety of recipes in this book that will show many different ways to prepare a few simple ingredients.

VEGETABLES AND FRUIT

Many vegetables and fruit can be carried for days without going bad and this makes them a viable option for camp cooking. But remember this: these fresh items hold lots in the way of liquid weight and take up some space in bulk, so there is the tradeoff. A dehydrated or otherwise preserved version of these foods will generally take up less weight and space. However, in most cases any fresh item will taste better than something preserved, as well as being more nutritious.

You will need to experiment with this a bit and much of your testing can be done at home before setting off. This is something that just has to be figured out over time by carrying such foods and observing their condition over days. Some things can be tested in the home by leaving food out much like you do bananas on the countertop and then seeing what happens, but this may not replicate exact conditions in the outdoors due to the controlled environment we create in the home.

Seasonality, humidity, temperature, and environment all affect how long these items last without refrigeration, but for me the best candidates that are commonplace for carrying fresh would be:

- Potatoes
- Carrots
- Apples
- Oranges
- Onions
- Zucchini
- Summer squash
- Other thick-skinned varieties of fruit and vegetables

The more fragile the food is to begin with, the more likely it is to bruise or go off before you have a chance to eat it. Delicate berries like blueberries and raspberries are better used as quickly as possible or picked wild and used in camp instead of carried in.

Dehydrating can be done in the home with modern dehydrators, and this makes a convenient way of packing these type foods. They can also be purchased dehydrated online and in specialty shops, as well as local groceries for some of them. Dried and dehydrated items will work in about all applications and have much less chance of spoilage over time.

When planning meals with fruit and vegetables, remember that storing leftovers can be a challenge—half a potato will go brown and spoil much sooner than a whole potato will! So try to use a whole item for your meal.

CURED MEATS

Cured meats like salt pork are a great addition to a camp pantry as a meat supplement, and salt-cured bacon has been a staple carry for woodsmen for several hundred years. These meats will last a good long time without refrigerants but are not commonplace in markets in most of the U.S. like they used to be.

Cured meats have had some combination of salt, sugar, and/or nitrates added to them to help preserve them. Curing meats also gives them an attractive flavor and color. Dry salt cures used to be common, and the process was called corning (which is why we have "corned beef"). Today salt water is often used and the process is called brining or pickling.

Cured and smoked hams can be very expensive to buy and time-consuming to make. However, again there is the tradeoff of very tasty and nutritious food that did not come from a package. It can be a great addition if conveyance is available.

Smithfield makes the most readily available cured bacon that can be packed and not refrigerated. Other sources can be found at local country butchers.

A single man can carry a couple of pounds of salt pork and eat well with just a few added sundries. There is absolutely something to be said for a couple slices of hot bacon and an ash cake with a good cup of coffee the morning before a hunt.

GRAINS

Many processed grains make excellent choices for the camp kitchen but the one I prefer most is farina, also known to every small child as Cream of Wheat. It makes a good meal when cooked with hot water and is easy to carry.

Many types of oats and oatmeal are also available and they make it easy to cook a filling and nutritious breakfast even if you have little in the way of cookware. Instant oats can be made just by adding hot water. Old-fashioned oats need to be boiled.

Oats and farina can also be added to many other recipes to make other meals, making these grains multifunctional, which to me is an important consideration. Carrying grains in the form of meal like cornmeal really makes a lot of sense. You can carry a JAW packet and use it like the raw ingredient. For example, corn bread mix can be made into an excellent cornmeal mush.

Grains I like include:

- Quaker Oats
- Nabisco Cream of Wheat
- Malt-O-Meal Hot Wheat Cereals

CREAM OF WHEAT PANCAKES

This is one of my favorite breakfast recipes, using one of my favorite grains.

1 egg
1½ cups milk
1 teaspoon oil (vegetable or corn)
1 cup all-purpose flour
2 teaspoons baking soda
½ teaspoon salt
¼ cup Cream of Wheat
Oil or lard for cooking (a few tablespoons)
Honey or syrup for serving

Mix ingredients except oil and honey/syrup. This should form a thick batter.

Add about a tablespoon of oil or lard to a skillet and heat to about medium over the fire. The skillet is ready when a drop of batter placed in the skillet sizzles.

Spoon about ¼ cup batter per pancake on the skillet. Cook until golden brown around the edges (2–3 minutes), then turn and cook until done (another 2–3 minutes). Add additional oil if needed to cook additional pancakes.

Serve with honey or syrup.

TIPS AND TRICKS

- Remember that hard cheeses like Cheddar don't have to be kept refrigerated but may not hold up well if carried in hot temperatures for long periods.
- Rinse all fruit and vegetables with water before using.
- While you might be tempted to cut up some of these foods ahead of time (like pineapple or melon), remember that you will have to keep cut-up fruit and vegetables cool,

which can be a challenge—particularly if you'll be out in the bush for an extended period.

- Nuts are another whole food and are easy to carry, store, and eat!
- Plan your meals ahead of time so you're not left with half-used fruit and vegetables that you have no way to store.

Chapter 4

SUPPLEMENTAL FOODSTUFFS

"Part of the secret of success in life is to eat what you like and let the food fight it out inside."

—MARK TWAIN

We've covered the basic building blocks of what you need to think about packing in—the main foods that will make up the bulk of your meals. But you will also want to think about packing in supplemental foodstuffs—items that will enhance your experience without adding too much bulk or take up too much space. For example, carrying dehydrated milk lets you fix a simple breakfast cereal without too much effort—and without having to light a fire.

BASIC INGREDIENTS

With all the types of food choices we have discussed prior to this point you may ask, "Why carry so many ingredients and powders like flour and baking powder?" Well, the simple answer is that there really is no need, especially for a shorter-term camp or trip.

However, there are some ingredients you'll want to carry even if you're planning to make most of your meals from JAW packets. One of these is salt. The other is baking soda. Its uses are so many as to make it worthwhile to carry even if you never cook with it.

Uses for baking soda:

- Toothpaste
- Dishwashing
- Dry shampoo
- Deodorant
- Stain removal
- Cleaning metal tools
- Antacid (medicinal)
- Treating insect bites (medicinal)

SPICES

I believe in carrying items that have a multiuse element and spices are no different. Many spices are also medicinal so your camp cupboard also becomes the medicine chest. Spices should be used on wild game very sparingly as they have a full flavor all their own that only requires a bit of salt in the end to make them very pleasing and palatable.

However, there are many uses in cooking with spices that help the body at the same time that they flavor our food:

- **Cayenne** has the ingredient capsaicin, which is used in many prescription and over-the-counter medicines to help relieve pain. It is believed to be an anti-inflammatory. If you're feeling a cold coming on, some cayenne sprinkled on your lunch can help reduce congestion.

- **Cinnamon** has antibacterial and anti-inflammatory properties. It can help improve blood sugar control and reduce triglycerides and total cholesterol, so it is thought to be heart-healthy.
- **Clove** is another spice with anti-inflammatory properties. It may also reduce cartilage and bone damage caused by arthritis. You can bite down on a clove to help reduce the pain from a toothache.
- **Coriander** can help calm digestive tract problems, like irritable bowel syndrome. It is also an antioxidant.
- **Garlic** is thought to help reduce cholesterol levels and has antioxidant properties. Garlic can be harvested wild in many areas of the U.S. in spring and summer. A good rule of thumb is to make sure the plant smells like garlic! If it doesn't, it probably isn't garlic and may be harmful to eat.
- **Ginger** is used in many cultures as an aid to digestion. It is also an anti-inflammatory and has shown promise in preventing migraines. Many people have found it helps with nausea.
- **Mustard** helps break up congestion (similar to cayenne) and making a footbath with a little mustard powder added to water can help treat athlete's foot.
- **Nutmeg** may have heart-protecting properties and it appears to kill certain cavity-causing microbes.
- **Sage** may protect the brain against Alzheimer's, according to several studies. It has anti-inflammatory and antioxidant properties.
- **Turmeric** is used in some cultures as an aid to digestion. It is also an anti-inflammatory.

See Chapter 18: Foraging, for more information on medicinal uses of herbs and other plants.

HONEY

Honey is almost a perfect food. It has so much nutritional value it could stand alone as a short-term survival food. It has the obvious benefit of lasting virtually forever—it has been found in Egyptian tombs and still viable to this day. It is a great source of daily energy and a fantastic medicine, making it multifunctional in the camp kitchen. It can replace any syrup for pancakes or biscuits and makes a great sugar replacement for teas and coffee.

BUSHCRAFT TIP

Honey has been used in medicine for thousands of years. It was used to treat wounds and infections. Some kinds of honey have been shown to have an antimicrobial property. Nowadays, honey is being used more and more frequently to help treat ulcers and skin infections.

COCOA, TEAS, AND COFFEE

Every campfire needs a kettle for water specifically being heated for one thing: the camper's favored drink. Nothing goes down better to many folks than a warm drink in the morning as well as after a nice evening meal. The best thing about beverages in general is that the main ingredient comes in powder form, making it easy to both store and carry.

What could be more traditional than hot cocoa around the campfire? Is there any better way to lift your spirits after a cold day? There are many types of hot cocoa mixes that will suit a camper's needs, and the chocolate flavoring can be added to other ingredients to make chocolate-flavored desserts, if you're of a mind to do so.

I prefer to carry a chocolate milk powder made from actual milk. I find the Country Cream brand works very well. It can be used in some other recipes calling for milk to add a chocolate twist—such as with cookies or breads and cereals like oatmeal and farina.

Many types of teas have medicinal or side benefits in addition to be being revitalizing and warming. Some herbal teas, like chamomile, can help you relax and unwind after a long day at camp. Most folks these days seem to prefer tea bags over brewing loose-leaf tea using a tea ball when camping out, but a tea ball allows you to make medicinal teas as well. Try out a few varieties at home before packing any along.

BUSHCRAFT TIP

Chaga (chaga mushroom) is a type of fungus that grows on birch trees. It has antiinflammatory and antioxidant properties and is thought to contain cancer-fighting compounds. Chaga can be used like any other tea and ground before adding boiling water to it or it can be used in a chunk and placed in a kettle of hot water to steep. In addition to its medicinal benefits, this naturally occurring fungus also makes a great fire tinder resource, being one of the few items that will ignite when dry with a low-temperature spark.

And we can't forget coffee. Coffee is an American tradition, as romantic as the cowboy era. A nice pot of hot coffee makes the weary camper rise to any morning occasion simply by the smell. What type of coffee you carry is a personal preference as is the form you carry (ground, instant, or beans). If you are a coffee drinker, far be it from me to tell you how to make it—everyone has a favorite method.

COWBOY COFFEE

*In its simplest form for camping and tramping
I prefer just ground coffee I can add to the pot.*

1 heaping tablespoon ground coffee per 1 cup water, adjusted to taste

Add coffee and water to a lidded pot or coffeepot and place over a hot fire. Bring to a boil.

Let the grounds settle, then add a bit of cold water to further settle the grounds. Pour and enjoy.

TIPS AND TRICKS

- Don't throw away used tea bags. Used tea bags can make an emergency first-aid item as a poultice, being astringent in nature.
- Old Bay Seasoning mix is one of my favorites. I use it in many recipes. Having a spice mix along cuts down on the number of individual spices I need to pack in.
- You can purchase citric acid in powder form to take the place of vinegar and lemon and lime juice.
- Carrying spices in their original containers can get bulky, so you can transfer them to labeled snack-sized storage bags, stackable pill containers (the kind you can buy at the drugstore), or any small plastic container you have on hand.
- You can reuse your coffee grounds a time or two, although the coffee gets progressively weaker, so you'll use more grounds per cup.

PART 2
Bushcraft
Cooking
Methods

Chapter 5

COOKING IN THE WILD

"There is no technique, there is just the way to do it. Now, are we going to measure or are we going to cook?"
—Frances Mayes, *Under the Tuscan Sun*

When I'm in camp, I don't necessarily break out a recipe book in order to make some tasty rabbit stew. I just use what I have on hand. So don't think you have to follow my recipes exactly or use the same ingredients I use. Think of the recipes in this book as a guide, not a rule. Here are some of my most important tips about cooking in the wild:

- Recipes are interchangeable. If you have a recipe you like for cooking red meat, then you can use it to cook raccoon.
- Think of opossum as pork. Whatever you do with that white meat, you can do with opossum.
- You can treat birds like chicken or turkey. If you've got a favorite chicken recipe, it'll probably work on a duck, too.

CHUCK BOX CONTENTS

The chuck box is your kitchen cabinet in the woods and is also your storage for these items when not in use. They have been known to Scouts for years as the patrol box and have also been called the grub box. This, along with the hearth, is the center of the camp cook's operations. This box was traditionally made from wood and is divided into smaller storage areas, sometimes with sliding boxes to be used as drawers when stood on end. Many of these boxes have folding or detachable legs to get them up higher for comfort in working, and the lid folds down to function as a work surface. See Figure 5.1.

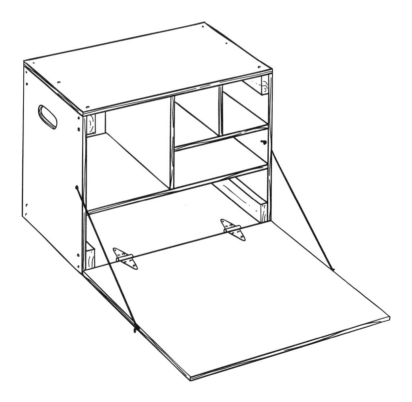

Figure 5.1 Chuck box

CONTAINERS AND SERVING WARE

- Dutch oven. A 2-quart version will feed 2 people.
- Steel skillet. An 8" will be good for 2 people; add 2" per person.
- Water container. This can be a canvas bucket to save space and should be at least 1 gallon per person.
- Measuring cup. This can be a dedicated device or improvised from your personal kit if graduations are on your cup or it is exactly 8 or 16 ounces.
- For serving, personal vessels can be used from backpacks or you can keep 1 small cup, bowl, and plate for each in the camp party.
- Eating utensils. Each member of the party should have a fork and spoon; these can be individually carried or kept as part of the chuck box.

COOK UTENSILS

If you are using cast-iron cookware, be sure to use wooden utensils, not metal, as metal can scratch the cast iron.

- Stirring spoon
- Serving spoon
- Spatula
- Whisk
- Camp knife
- Oven mitt
- Ladle

EXTRAS

- Cutting board
- Leather gloves
- Lid lifter for the Dutch oven
- Trivet (a 6" version works well for most needs)

- Marinade syringe
- Natural bristle scrub brush

FOODSTUFFS FOR THE CHUCK BOX

Most of the things I carry on the trail for quick cooking are in dry form. This saves water weight in the pack, and then water is added from a more localized source.

- I always carry beef and chicken bouillon powder. It's light and adds great flavor to soups and stews.
- Stews and gravies can be thickened using potatoes, evaporated milk, or powdered eggs. Be flexible; if you don't plan to use evaporated milk for other cooking, then don't bring it. Plan on using potatoes or powdered eggs in your stews instead.
- Self-rising flour should always be carried as this avoids the need for yeast.
- A seasoning mix or Old Bay can be used as a replacement for any other series of spices and even for plain salt. It also works for making jerky and for smoking meats, so it is a good resource to carry.
- Animal fats can be used to replace oils and lard. Remember that the fat of wild game will be similar to another animal of the same meat coloration, so opossum is most similar to suet and deer and raccoon are similar to lard.

COMMON SUBSTITUTIONS

If a recipe calls for an ingredient you don't have with you, you may be able to find a reasonable substitute in your pack or in the environment around you. For example, chicory or roasted dandelion root can be steeped to make a good coffee substitute.

SIMPLE INGREDIENT SUBSTITUTIONS

Ingredient	Amount	Substitute
Beef or chicken broth	1 cup	1 tablespoon soy sauce + 1 cup water less 1 tablespoon
Cheese	Any amount	Cheeses with similar texture and moisture content like Cheddar, Colby, and Monterey jack can be used interchangeably, as can cheeses like Parmesan, Asiago, and Romano
Chocolate		1 ounce unsweetened chocolate (1 square) is equivalent to $\frac{1}{4}$ cup cocoa powder; 1 cup semisweet chocolate chips is equal to 1 cup other flavored chips or 1 cup chopped nuts or 1 cup dried fruit
Cream of . . . soup	1 can	Any cream of . . . soup can be interchanged—cream of mushroom can be substituted for cream of celery; cream of chicken can be used in place of cream of mushroom, etc.
Corn syrup	1 cup	$1\frac{1}{4}$ cups granulated sugar plus $\frac{1}{3}$ cup water; or 1 cup honey
Dried fruit	Any amount	Raisins, dried currants, dried cranberries, and pitted prunes can be used interchangeably
Egg	1 whole egg (about 3 tablespoons)	$2\frac{1}{2}$ tablespoons powdered egg plus $2\frac{1}{2}$ tablespoons water; or 3 tablespoons mayonnaise
Fats	$\frac{1}{2}$ cup	$\frac{1}{2}$ cup butter is equivalent to $\frac{1}{2}$ cup less 1 tablespoon vegetable oil or $\frac{1}{2}$ cup shortening or lard
Flour, self-rising	1 cup	$\frac{7}{8}$ cup all-purpose flour plus $1\frac{1}{2}$ teaspoons baking powder and $\frac{1}{2}$ teaspoon salt
Grains	Any amount (cooked)	White rice, brown rice, wild rice, barley, and bulgur can all be used interchangeably
Herbs		1 tablespoon chopped fresh herbs is equivalent to 2 teaspoons dried herbs
Honey	1 cup	$1\frac{1}{4}$ cups granulated sugar plus $\frac{1}{3}$ cup water

TIPS AND TRICKS

- If you have room in your pack, aluminum foil is a handy item to have along. Wrap some leftovers in it, place in hot coals, and in 15 minutes you've got a nice warm meal.
- Use disposable water bottles to carry liquids, like vegetable oil. For smaller amounts of liquid, use the small plastic containers meant for carrying on shampoo and soap. These are readily available at drugstores.
- Test out recipes and substitutions at home before hitting the trail. This can help you make adjustments before you leave.
- For shorter trips, consider packing premeasured ingredients for each meal in a storage bag. This simplifies the cooking process, and you won't have to pack in measuring cups and spoons.
- If you camp a lot, dehydrating food at home can help you save on weight and bulk.

— Chapter 6 —
BUILDING A FIRE

"The glories of a mountain campfire are far greater than may be guessed . . . One can make a day of any size, and regulate the rising and setting of his own sun and the brightness of its shining."

—John Muir

Fire is the key element to a successful outdoor adventure. Without fire we are at the mercy of the sun to do our cooking unless we happen to be camped on a lava field, so the first priority is learning to make a proper fire.

Cook fires are different from campfires, signal fires, or warming fires, and they must be built and handled in accordance with the way we will cook our food.

A fire requires three elements: heat, oxygen, and fuel. If any of these elements is missing or is not in the proper amount, the fire will dwindle or die out.

PICKING THE RIGHT WOOD

The first consideration in building a fire is to choose what type of wood to collect. Which you choose depends on what kind of fire you're making:

- Softwoods (such as cedar) are for starting fires.
- Hardwoods (such as oak) are for sustaining fires and cooking fires.
- Resinous woods (such as pine and spruce) make great campfires and signal fires but they make horrible cook fires and can impart a bad flavor to anything the smoke comes into contact with.

So to that end we must first understand a bit about wood in general. There are really two types of trees:

1. **Deciduous:** those that lose their leaves every year
2. **Coniferous:** those with needles; for the most part these trees lose needles all year long and replace them with new ones

A deciduous tree is not always a hardwood, and a conifer is not always a softwood. To add to the confusion both types of trees can have resins, or oils, that impart bad taste to food, especially meat being cooked directly over flame or coals. So how do you tell the difference if you are not a tree guru? The answer can be a fairly simple deduction in most cases.

First, stay away from any coniferous tree except for lighting the initial fire. Feed no coniferous fuels. For deciduous trees (non-birch species), split the piece you plan to use and try to impress a fingernail into the wood. If you leave a mark, then don't use the wood, unless it is for quick fire starting. Softer woods will ignite much faster, but hardwoods will create much better cooking coals and fires. See the following table for more information on the various BTUs put out by different types of wood.

BTUS FOR WOOD BURNING

Species	Heat per Cord (Million BTUs)	% of Green Ash	Ease of Splitting	Smoke	Sparks	Coals	Fragrance	Overall Quality
Black locust	27.9	140	Difficult	Low	Few	Excellent	Slight	Excellent
Black walnut	22.2	111	Easy	Low	Few	Good	Good	Excellent
Bur oak	26.2	131	Easy	Low	Few	Excellent	Good	Excellent
Eastern red cedar	18.2	91	Medium	Medium	Many	Poor	Excellent	Fair
Honey locust	26.7	133	Easy	Low	Few	Excellent	Slight	Excellent
Larch (tamarack)	21.8		Easy-med		Many	Fair	Slight	Fair
Lodgepole pine	21.1		Easy		Many	Fair	Good	Fair
Maple (other)	25.5	128	Easy	Low	Few	Excellent	Good	Excellent
Mulberry	25.8	129	Easy	Medium	Many	Excellent	Good	Excellent
Osage orange	32.9	165	Easy	Low	Many	Excellent	Excellent	Excellent
Ponderosa pine	16.2	81	Easy	Medium	Many	Fair	Good	Fair
Red oak	24.6	123	Medium	Low	Few	Excellent	Good	Excellent
Rocky Mountain juniper	21.8	109	Medium	Medium	Many	Poor	Excellent	Fair

BTUS FOR WOOD BURNING

Species	Heat per Cord (Million BTUs)	% of Green Ash	Ease of Splitting	Smoke	Sparks	Coals	Fragrance	Overall Quality
Silver maple	19.0	95	Medium	Low	Few	Excellent	Good	Excellent
Spruce	15.5	78	Easy	Medium	Many	Poor	Slight	Fair
Sycamore	19.5	98	Difficult	Medium	Few	Good	Slight	Good
White oak	29.1	146	Medium	Low	Few	Excellent	Good	Excellent
Willow	17.6	88	Easy	Low	Few	Poor	Slight	Poor

STARTING THE FIRE

Once you know what type of wood to use, your next step is to understand the basics of building a fire. The key to starting a fire is simple: gather lots of tinder, lots of kindling, and lots of fuel.

- Tinder is highly combustible materials. This could be inner bark, dead weeds, or fine shavings from larger material. Often the best tinder for *starting* a fire is a heavily resin-laden wood, like pine, or bark from trees containing oils, such as birch. Again these are for starting the fire, not maintaining it.
- Kindling is small dry sticks from pencil lead to pencil size. Quickly establishing a fire requires lots of surface area of combustible material, so using lots of smaller pieces of kindling will help you establish your fire.
- Fuel is hardwood that is thumb-sized to 2" in diameter.

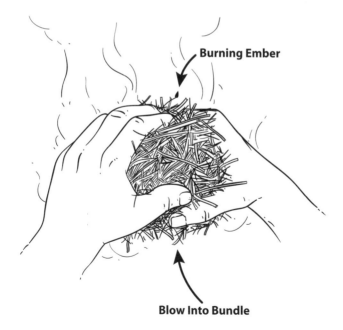

Burning Ember

Blow Into Bundle

Figure 6.1 Tinder bundle

Make sure your selected area for the fire affords protection from high wind and allows for ease of maintenance. Make sure that the area you plan to build the fire is dry. If the ground is damp, place a layer of dry sticks on the ground to keep the base of the fire dry, lest it suffer from conductive heat loss and evaporative moisture, making it much harder to keep the fire going.

Next, process your tinder materials as fine as possible. This is a critical element that makes many folks fail in the earliest stage of fire building. Again you want the maximum surface area to give you the best chance of ignition.

Place a tinder bundle on the ground if it is dry or on the tinder base you created if it is wet. See Figure 6.1 for an example of a tinder bundle.

Now take another good handful of kindling and gently place it over the pile of tinder. Don't overcomplicate this by building a Lincoln Logs–style home. Just ensure the sticks have plenty of air space between them. Crisscross as much as you can, building up not out. Fire loves chaos! See Figure 6.2 for an example of a fire lay.

Figure 6.2 Fire lay

1. Once you have set your fire lay, you are ready for ignition. Make sure you have at least as much or more tinder set aside as you have used to build the initial lay and 2 times that much fuel before proceeding to lighting the fire.

2. Once ready, you can ignite the base of the tinder material. A good space should be left open for this operation to allow good flow of oxygen from the bottom to create updraft from heat rising and pulling air into the fire from the bottom.

3. Once the fire begins to burn do not rush to add more material. A simple rule is: only add kindling when the flames have risen above the current level of fuel. This will prevent you from suffocating the fire through lack of oxygen.

4. Once the fire is established and kindling is burned, you may begin to add fuel to maintain the fire. It is a complicated-sounding process but gets easier each time you do it. Remember that wet or damp wood will starve the fire of oxygen through evaporation and also reduce heat. If your fuel is marginal, add more slowly and use more kindling as needed to increase heat. Place damp fuels near the fire to begin drying and remember to split any damp wood at least once to expedite the drying process and possibly expose dry wood inside.

After building a fire as outlined, you can immediately place a kettle or pot of water on to boil. Once the kindling becomes coals, you are ready for the pan and frying. This fire will last about 20 minutes or so and is perfect for a quick lunch stop and hot meal.

TESTING THE HEAT OF THE COALS

You will want to have a good guess as to the heat of the fire especially for baking and roasting, so here is a simple way to make a good guess. Place your hand above the coal bed at cooking level and count the seconds you can comfortably hold it there with your palm down toward the fire:

- 5 seconds = low
- 4 seconds = medium
- 3 seconds = medium-high
- 2 seconds = high

If you have the means, the surest way to tell if your meat is fully cooked is to use a thermometer placed in the thickest part of the meat to verify it has reached safe temperatures. If you do not have a meat thermometer, it's better to cook in a way that ensures thorough cooking, like boiling or stewing. At a minimum cook the meat until it is an even color down to the bone and there is no sign of pink or blood.

MINIMUM SAFE TEMPERATURE FOR MEAT AND FISH	
MEAT	**MINIMUM**
Pork	160°F
Beef	145°F
Lamb	160°F
Chicken	165°F
Duck	165°F
Fish	145°F
Most game (deer, elk)	145°F
Rabbit and other small game	160°F

ADVANCED FIRE CRAFT

Fire is the tool that many consider only second in importance to a good cutting tool. Fire is a main tool for combating cold-weather injury as well as general comfort around camp in cold environments. It will disinfect water, cook and preserve food, make medicines, keep bugs at bay . . . and the list goes on.

SOURCES OF IGNITION

Plenty of items on the market today—from actual lighters to road flares—will almost always ensure a flame to ignite even marginal tinder sources. You should have three methods to effect ignition at all times: lighter, ferrocerium rod, and sun glass or magnifying lens. I have not included matches on this list as it is my belief that matches really can do nothing we cannot accomplish with these three methods. Matches are not a value-added item, especially for the inherent issues one may face when using them, like moisture, wind, and gross motor dexterity when you're cold. However, matches should be practiced along with any method of fire starting in case you have those and nothing else.

The other two most important methods of fire starting to understand are the bow-and-drill and flint-and-steel methods. Both of these methods can be effected from material in the landscape provided you have not lost your high-carbon blade from the sheath on your hip. (You should always have some type of retention for your blade so that this is not a possibility.)

THE BOW-AND-DRILL FIRE METHOD

The bow-and-drill kit can be made using only stone or glass tools but a knife makes the job much more convenient. There are those that would tell you that to truly practice a primitive skill you must always use primitive tools, and there is something to be said for improvising tools from the landscape, but these days it is not hard to find materials like metal and glass to work with.

Bow-and-Drill Kit

The bow-and-drill method is basically the idea of rubbing two sticks together to create a friction spark. However, it is slightly more complex than that and requires a number of elements to work. You will need four things in your kit:

1. Bow and bowstring
2. Spindle (also called the drill)
3. Hearth board
4. Bearing block (also called the handhold)

Except for the rope (ideally made of nylon), all of the items in this kit can be made from the landscape but it's easier to make the kit ahead of time to carry with you. See Figure 6.3 for what this kit looks like.

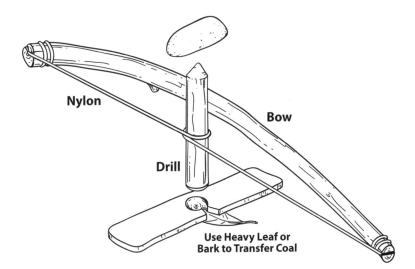

Figure 6.3 Bow-and-drill fire kit

The basic technique is to wind the spindle into the bow-string in the bow, then rotate the spindle against the hearth board, using a handhold to keep the hearth in place. Doing this, you create an ember, a smoldering coal that will need to be added to a bird's nest of combustible materials.

Remember, we need heat, oxygen, and fuel to effect ignition or make the smoldering coal. So our set must be made to take maximum advantage of all three of these inputs. Survival is like a manufacturing process: All inputs will affect the output, in this case the burning coal. Any variation must be avoided to control the correct output. Understanding this, we need to ensure many things at the same time; without certain inputs, in the correct order, we will not get the desired output.

Creating the Bow-and-Drill Kit

When these components are used correctly they will make a simple machine that causes dust to accumulate. That dust is then heated by the drill's friction on the board. Choosing the correct components, using the right form, and understanding when and how much pressure and speed to apply are the key inputs to the process. The only variation should be the materials you select, which can be controlled for the most part.

The hearth and spindle can be made from the same wood. It should be a softer wood, one that you can leave a fingernail impression in by pushing down. Examples of good woods to select are poplar, cedar, willow, and pine. The wood for these two components must be as dry as you can manage to find but should not be in a state of decay. My preference for this material would be tulip poplar, as the lower branches will often be hanging dead from the tree and be off the ground and dry, barring a few days of hard rain.

Generally speaking you want your hearth board about as long as your forearm and as thick as your thumb when finished, so select a limb or piece of wood larger than this so it can be split down to make a flat board of these dimensions. The spindle of the same material can be made from a branch as well and need only be about thumb diameter and the length of the span from your outstretched thumb to your pinky; a bit longer will not hurt as you will be carving both ends.

See Figures 6.4 and 6.5 for examples of what the spindle and hearth board look like.

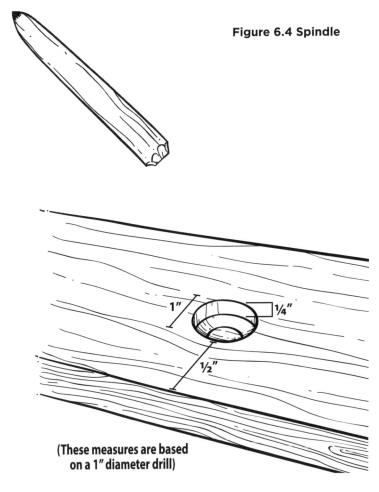

Figure 6.4 Spindle

1"

¼"

½"

(These measures are based on a 1" diameter drill)

Figure 6.5 Hearth board

The bearing block should be made from the hardest wood available. Hickory and beech are good selections. Choose a green sapling if one is available, about 3" diameter. Cut a chunk 4–5" in length, then split ⅓ off of one side with your knife.

See Figure 6.6 for an example of a bearing block.

Figure 6.6 Bearing block

As to the bow, this can be made from any branch and does not have to even be bent like a bow. It just needs to be fairly stiff so as not to bend or break under strain and should be about ½" diameter by 3' long. The longer the bow is, the fewer strokes it takes to make revolutions of the spindle. A mistake I see a lot is using a bow well under 3'. To create the bow is as simple as tying a string to a branch. I have found a fork on one end of the stick and a loop works best with a simple stake notch on the other end to tie it off with a straight lashing and a clove hitch. The string need not be so tight that the bow must bend to load the spindle but cannot be so loose that the drill slips under downward pressure either. See Figure 6.7 for an example of the bow.

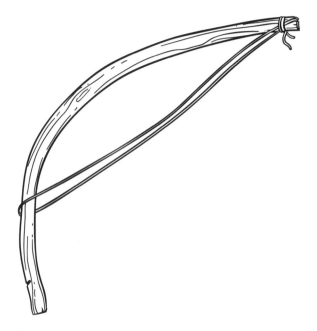

Figure 6.7 Bow

The bird's nest must be made up of coarse, medium, and fine materials. The true beauty of this is that most of the materials good for making the hearth and spindle will also provide the materials for a bird's nest. The inner bark of the poplar, bark from the cedar, or inner bark of the willow are all great candidates for this. There are lots of other items that can be used within the bird's nest, such as shredded birch barks, small dead pine needles, and other things with a natural accelerant or highly combustible oils, which will aid after the flame is created.

Do not use too much dry grass or leaves, as these items burn quickly and the bird's nest must have longevity when burning to ignite the rest of the fire lay materials. Processing is the name of the game when constructing the bird's nest. Shred barks to obtain lots of the finest materials you can. Always put out something to catch the droppings as you process the material, as many times the finest material will drop to the ground. The back of your knife can do much of the work if the material is still attached to the branch or the tree when you are collecting it. If these materials are wet when being collected, process them immediately, as the more surface area you create the faster it will dry. See Figure 6.8 for an example of a bird's nest.

Figure 6.8 Bird's nest

If the sun is shining, place the materials in the sun, spread out as much as possible on a dark surface such as a tarp. Once these materials are dry they can be fashioned to look like a bird's nest—and that is exactly how it should look. You should take a look at old bird's nests when possible to see how they are constructed. They will have finer material in the middle or center and progressively coarser materials to the outside.

To prep the spindle for use, make it as straight and round as possible. The back of your knife can finely shave small materials to achieve this if an area of the spindle is slightly bent or crooked. Once it is straight and round, prepare the ends for use. One end of the drill should look like a worn eraser on a pencil, slightly rounded but still flat. This end will be on the hearth board to create maximum surface area and friction. This is where you want all the friction to be between the spindle and the hearth. The top of the spindle or drill needs to be shaped like the lead side of a pencil that needs sharpening: slightly dull yet still somewhat pointed. You want as little friction as possible on the top of the spindle, as this will make it easier to push and pull the bow; keep the friction on the bottom, where it belongs.

The bearing block is a key part of the set and probably the least understood, as it causes the most problems for many people. Using a hardwood for this is critical if you are making a set completely from the landscape. Softwood will immediately begin to wear away, causing the spindle to rub the wrong way. This is called "shouldering out," and it is the biggest failure point for beginners who do not realize why they are getting worn out from operating the set and why they cannot get the set to run smoothly or get enough pressure down on the spindle.

Putting the Kit Together
Using your knife, create a small divot in the middle of the bearing block on the flat side. It only needs to be large enough to accept the point of the spindle. A free-spinning drill will be

smooth and easy to operate. If you are having problems, this is the first place to look.

Then load the spindle onto the bowstring. When the spindle is loaded it should be on the outside of the string so that no friction occurs within the bow itself.

Create a small divot just off center of the hearth to accept the spindle. Do not make this divot very deep, as you don't want to waste material you will need to form a coal. It only needs to guide the spindle during the burn-in process.

After loading the spindle to the bow, burn an area of the hearth board to guide you in notch construction. A proper notch should be a V cut in which the bottom of the V goes approximately ⅛" into the burned area. The angles of the V should be between 30° and 45°, approximately. This notch is very important in forming the coal. It gives the dust an area to accumulate from the drilling process and keeps it confined, which helps the material gather heat and lets in just enough oxygen to make it smolder as an ember if the rest of the process is performed correctly.

Place the spindle on the divot. If possible you always want the notch to the front of the board facing away from you. This will allow you to easily view the process when operating the drill. Begin to apply enough downward pressure to hold the drill in the divot as you slowly rotate the spindle. This is important as it will marry the drill to the divot for when you begin to create the coal. You don't need speed at this point; downward pressure will create enough friction to begin burning the wood if you use the entire bow with steady strokes.

Once the wood has burned around the spindle and things are running smooth you need to stop, as again any waste of material now reduces what you have to make a coal later. When making the notch or the area that the coal will form, take care. You do not want it too narrow, as this will clog up as well as limit oxygen to the ember. Yet it cannot be too big, as the oxygen must be properly controlled and the dust somewhat compact.

Inspect all components now before beginning to attempt a coal. Check the bowstring for stretch and retighten if necessary. Check your bearing block to make sure the divot is not getting deep and the spindle has not begun to shoulder out. Deal with these issues now, or they will only get worse.

After this you are ready to begin making fire with sticks! Okay, you need one little extra item that makes things much easier in the end and may save a good coal from going out due to ground moisture. You need to make a welcome mat that your coal is going to flow onto from the notch. This can be a small sliver of bark or a thin piece of wood, but it should be two times as wide as the notch and goes under the hearth board to catch the coal.

Creating the Coal

Assume the proper position: bent over on one knee, with the front foot on the hearth board close to the spindle but not touching and causing friction. The other leg should have the knee resting comfortably on the ground parallel to your body but tucked inside enough not to interfere with the bow moving forward and back during the drilling process.

Make sure the crook of your wrist is locked into your shin so that the spindle will not move side to side. Make sure there are no obstructions that will interfere with the full movement of the bow. Lean forward to put steady downward pressure on the spindle with the bearing block. You should have your chest over your knee at this point and easily be able to observe the activity in the notch. Begin to operate the bow again slowly at first to maintain a rhythm. You don't need speed yet; you want steady, long strokes and downward pressure using the entire length of the bow.

The goal at this point is to remove material from the board and the drill and fill the notch with a dark brown fluffy material. Many folks make the mistake of trying to go too fast, assuming speed will make an ember, but if there is no dust in the notch you have no fuel to create the ember.

After several strokes you will see some smoke and the notch should begin to fill with material. Once that material begins to spill forward in front of the notch you can increase the cadence of your bow strokes, going 2–3 times faster. It should only take about 10–12 full strokes of the bow at this point to create a burning coal.

When you stop, don't do it suddenly and with a jerk as this may disturb the coal you created. Instead, slow down during the last couple of strokes and stop in the same position you started. Slowly remove the spindle and bow and observe the coal. If it seems to be smoking outside the board where the dust has gathered, you are probably home free. Don't get excited, as you have a lot of time to turn the ember into a fire—about 5 minutes or more in reality. You can slowly lift the board at an angle and tap it gently with the spindle to dislodge any material that may be clogged in the notch. If the coal is still smoking at this point, you can sit back and relax for a minute, catch a few breaths, and smile!

Turning the Coal Into Fire

Now comes the most important part of the operation. Bring the bird's nest to the coal (never the other way around). Tilt the nest toward the welcome mat and pick up the welcome mat, moving it to the nest. Slowly tap the welcome mat to dump the coal into the nest. This should be a tiny drop—about a ¼" at most.

Slightly fold the nest and begin to add some oxygen by breathing into it slightly—not hard blows, just light breaths. If the coal is still burning strong you can raise the nest, slightly tilted, so that you are blowing up into it and the heat rises into the bulk of the nest. As the ember grows, smoke will begin to roll from the back side of the nest. This is the cue for you to blow a bit harder. As the smoke thickens you can increase the oxygen until it begins to burn.

Once the nest flames, turn it over so the flames are on the bottom and heat rises to the non-burning material. Place it into your fire lay and make fire!

FLINT-AND-STEEL METHOD

Why is this an important method for us to understand? For the same reason the bow-and-drill method is important, in case we would lose the majority of our gear. We do not want to make two bow-and-drill fires if we can help it, so we make charred material as soon as we have the first fire. Then a flint-and-steel fire can be made the next time round.

Charred material will only require a simple spark to ignite into an ember. It can be ignited from many possible sources, but the flint-and-steel method is the number one best way if open flame devices are unavailable. As long as we do not lose our primary cutting tool, we should be able to find a rock to serve as the flint.

To effect this method you will need to drive small shards of iron material from the back of your knife with a rock. These particles will combust with friction and oxygen at 800°F. It may take some searching for a rock that will do this but any flint, chert, or quartz rock will work if you can break or find a sharp edge. See Figure 6.9 for an example of a flint-and-steel kit.

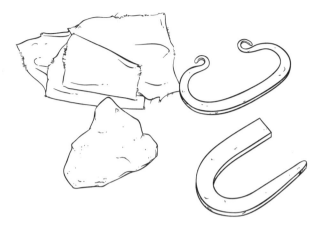

Figure 6.9 Flint-and-steel kit

Material for Flint-and-Steel Ignition

Some fungi like chaga (true tinder fungus) will take the spark from this method without charring first. You can also get the dust from some types of shelf fungus (*Fomes fomentarius*) to take a spark. To accomplish this you'll need to create a small pile of dust with a saw cut or by scraping with the back of a knife. Once the dust has ignited it must be left to grow into a coal, whereas the true tinder fungus can be ignited within a larger piece and the dust is not necessary. With either of these materials you want the softer inner materials, not the outer hard surface.

You can also elect to char material, which is a much better guarantee that a spark will give you ignition. This material can be made from many things from the landscape, including punky decaying wood and the inner pith from some plants like mullein. You can also use materials that are 100 percent cotton, such as from clothing or kit.

Making Char

To make charred material of any kind means you will need to severely limit the oxygen to a material that is contained and superheated. The easiest way to do this is to use some type of metal chamber with a way for gases to escape as it heats up the material inside.

A stainless steel bottle and nesting cup will work for this, as will an old can with a flat rock as a lid. Place the material to be charred inside the chamber and place the chamber into the fire. Coals are better for this than direct flame, but either will work.

As the material is heated in the chamber, gas that looks like smoke will begin to escape from any place that is not completely sealed. This is okay as long as oxygen cannot enter. Once the smoke stops the charring should be complete. It is very important to wait until the chamber is completely cool before opening the container, as the addition of oxygen to hot material will make it burn.

Once the container is cool, inspect the contents. If it is black and frail looking, it is most likely correct. If it is brown, it can be put back into the fire the same way without harm. It is easy enough to test a small amount of the material to make sure it is correct. Many woodsmen will carry a specific tin for fire material and charring called a char tin. Altoids breath mint–type tins or old shoe polish cans work well for this.

If you are using this type of system, sparks can be struck from the metal tool directly into the tin, so that the surface area to catch an ember is increased. Once an ember is created it will need to be placed into a bird's nest as described in the previous section on the bow-and-drill method.

Advantages of Char

There are many advantages to charring material. Making a highly combustible material that can be added to marginal materials within a bird's nest allows extended heat sources for effecting ignition. Charred material can be ignited with almost any spark, from old lighters to ferrocerium rods to a sun glass. This variety of ignition methods makes char a perfect material to keep in good supply within your kit.

SOLAR FIRE

There is a huge advantage to using a sun glass to create an ember: The sun is a renewable resource, and you are expending no resource from your kit to make this ember. All materials for ember-making can be collected from the wild and are not difficult to use. Remember the discussion on adding a burning ember to a bird's nest? This will not change, nor will the construction of the nest itself. Any charred material can be ignited by the sun glass, as can both of the fungus species we have discussed. Horse hoof fungus may work better as a dust but it will make a nice coal in a short amount of time. You can also create an ember by compressing natural materials like cattail down or poplar bark into a tight small ball about ¼" in diameter, then using the glass to burn into the material, creating a smoldering ember.

TIPS AND TRICKS

- You should always be thinking of the next fire. If you use up your emergency fuel source, what will you do for the next fire? That's why I suggest making char as a priority from the first fire.
- Remember, campfire cooking is done over coals, not flame. Cooking over a flame will char the outside of your food while leaving the inside cold. Cook over the coals for better results for most meals.

- While you're eating, put a pot of water on the fire so that water will be hot for cleanup.
- Cover pots when cooking. This helps meals cook faster and keeps insects from getting too curious.
- Be patient. Since you'll do most of your cooking over coals, not open flame, you have to wait for the fire to die down. It will also take longer to cook a meal over a fire than in an oven or on a stove.
- Keep an eye out. Most foods cooked over a fire will need your attention from time to time. You'll need to stir it often and move it to different parts of the fire (or move hotter coals underneath your pot) in order to cook evenly and thoroughly. A fire is not like an oven or a stove; the heat will not be evenly distributed.

Chapter 7

TOOLS AND UTENSILS

"Real freedom lies in wildness, not in civilization."

—CHARLES LINDBERGH

Cooking requires equipment—everything from knives to cut meat to pots to cook it in to plates to serve it on. But to carry all that equipment would take up a lot of room and a lot of weight. In this chapter, we'll talk about what equipment you really need, how you can lighten your load, and what tools and utensils you can actually make from materials in your environment.

Almost any tool you could possibly need for processing and cooking food can be made from the landscape in a pinch for sure. However, the most difficult to make—especially depending on local resources and skill level—are cutting tools and containers. Peripheral items, from cutting boards to spoons and spatulas, are easy enough to improvise if you need to.

COOKING EQUIPMENT MATERIALS

Before we get into actually choosing and using containers, we should discuss material types a bit to have a better understanding of the pros and cons depending on the situation and the way we are using it. Obviously we can fashion utensils from natural materials and improvise cookware from cans, which we'll describe later in this chapter. But for this discussion, let's start off with talking of dedicated containers we may carry for cooking that are bought new or used and the types of materials they are made from.

We will not speak to cooking with tin and copper in this book although for re-enactment purposes they are a viable option. However, brass buckets make a good addition if you can't afford the heavy stainless steel kind. Brass buckets can often be found at estate sales and antique malls at reasonable prices.

CAST IRON

The biggest advantage to cast iron is even heating. It takes time to heat this material but it retains heat well and cooks food evenly due to this property. Cold spots caused by a sudden change in wind direction will be rare if ever. Lots of great cookware is made from cast iron, from ovens to pans, griddles, and biscuit and bread pans.

One of things most often carried in westward expansion where wagons were available was the family's cast iron, especially the Dutch oven. Because these come in many sizes from 1 quart to as large as 14" across, they can be fitted well to your needs and form of conveyances.

The biggest downside from a traveling standpoint is weight. Cast iron also requires a certain amount of care for it to maintain its seasoning and keep food from sticking.

SHEET STEEL

Sheet steel, both thick and thin, has been used for making cookware since as long as it has been available. Steel is generally lighter than cast iron but still heavy unless the gauge is thin. Many nice old cold-handle skillets are available; they make great camp cooking tools that weigh very little compared to cast iron and will season much like cast iron, since they're made of a porous metal. Rust is the main enemy of this material (much like cast iron) so some care must be taken to maintain it.

ENAMELWARE

Enameled cookware came to the U.S. around 1850. Americans began to own enamel-lined culinary utensils, but they were very plain—nothing like the colourful mottled surfaces that were yet to come. The Stuart & Peterson foundry in Philadelphia was making enamel-lined cast-iron pots in the 1860s.

Enamelware is an iconic part of camp cooking, and it is still as viable an option today as it was in the late nineteenth and early twentieth centuries. It is lightweight, easy to clean, transfers heat well, and has few drawbacks. The main issue is the chipping that occurs from abuse. But drinking vessels from this material are hard to beat for a good cup of morning coffee. It can be found in good condition, is cheap enough, and will last a lifetime if cared for.

STAINLESS STEEL

An improvement over carbon steel in both strength and rust resistance, stainless is by far one of my personal favorites for camp cookware. It will never cook as well as cast iron in my opinion, but the tradeoff in terms of weight and maintenance alone gives it high marks for use over time and seasons.

It transfers heat fairly well, although not as well as cast iron. While camping I often use sand straight from the creek bed to scrub my stainless steel, and it is none the worse for wear. Stainless steel is getting less and less expensive, so it is generally very affordable. There are very fancy pieces on the market that combine stainless steel with copper or aluminum bottoms for better heat transfer but these are not necessary for simple camp meals.

ALUMINUM

Let me first say that until I see conclusive research that cooking in aluminum has major issues on health I will continue to use it. However, each person should make his or her own judgments about this material. It has so many advantages from a weight and cost standpoint it is hard to ignore. Hundreds of thousands of Boy and Girl Scouts have cooked with aluminum cook sets for the past 80-plus years; these sets are readily available and cheap to buy.

Aluminum has fantastic conductivity and is very durable and lightweight. Modern anodized aluminum takes away the concerns of health risks, is inexpensive to buy, and gives a helpful nonstick surface to cook on as well. The only issue is from scratching, as with most other nonstick coatings.

There are even Dutch ovens made from aluminum that are a third the weight of cast iron. Aluminum transfers heat very well, so coffee cups of this material make drinking hot coffee a dangerous game.

TITANIUM

Titanium is the latest and greatest material for camp cookware, but is it the best? In my opinion this fantastic metal, used for making the lightest of modern cookware, is a great resource. If you are counting every ounce in the pack, that is where the advantages begin and end for me. The drawbacks are that titanium is very expensive, tends to warp in the direct heat of a campfire, and it does not cook evenly at all. Like aluminum, it's a good heat conductor so it heats too fast and cools too fast for cooking.

For simply cooking, like preparing a prepackaged mix with water meal, and combined with a fuel-based camp stove, they have their place for sure, but for actual camping and bush-craft, I feel the expense far outweighs the usefulness.

BASIC EQUIPMENT

Let's first discuss the minimum equipment you need and how you can make one item serve several purposes. A water bottle and nesting cup of metal will prepare a lot of food for one person, and a good belt knife will help with processing both food and fire fuels. Some water bottles that have cups also come with a lid for the cup and have been further developed to allow the cup to be suspended by a makeshift bail, becoming a small pot.

You can use a flattened stick to stir anything in a simple one-pot meal and a forked green stick will suffice for a fork. If you don't want to improvise a utensil, you can carry a spoon easy enough. If you want to carry a fork as well, this takes little room and there are plenty of combination spoon/fork utensils on the market. With this minimal kit, you can make any of the one-pot recipes in this book by adjusting ingredient levels, or you can easily prepare a few packaged foods into several different meals. For traveling light and a single person on the trail, this kit is hard to beat for a weekend outing. See Figure 7.1 for an example of a bottle kit with nesting cup that can be used as a bush pot.

Figure 7.1 Bottle kit

For a longer stay or if you have an extra person along, a communal pot that's a bit larger will come in handy—for heating water if nothing else. Something in the 2-quart range is good. This can be a commercial bush-type pot with lid and a bail handle that allows it to be hung over the coals. A simple stainless milking bucket will also work well—milking buckets also have bail handles but no lids.

BUSHCRAFT TIP

To me the best folding cook sets are always the plain BSA aluminum sets with the handle that holds the unit together and a wingnut that secures it.

SINGLE-POT COOKING

Single-pot cooking has been very popular for a long time both from an ease of cleanup and prep standpoint, but also from the necessity of only carrying one container for cooking when trail hiking, camping, or trekking. The one pot can range from a simple #10 can and a bailing wire bail (handle) to a bucket of some sort or even a readymade bush pot or small cylindrical coffeepot. Any of these apparatus will work, giving you many advantages. A larger pot can make it easier to carry water to camp, boil that water for disinfection, and cook anything from coffee or tea to simple one-pot meals that can be adapted from almost any foods available.

TWO-POT ALTERNATIVE

Single-container cooking can also be done in a pan or skillet but to carry these without the pot is a bit counterintuitive to be honest as it negates the larger capacity for boiling water in camp. However combining the two (pot and skillet) gives you a fantastic variety of meals that you can accomplish, and if the pan nests somehow to create a lid you have a further advantage.

THE DUTCH OVEN

The most famous of the one-pot meal makers is the Dutch oven, and these prized items, passed on from generation to generation, are the king of camp cooking. There is nothing you can make on the stove or in the oven at home that cannot be accomplished with a good Dutch oven.

If you are unfamiliar with it, a Dutch oven is a cast-iron pot with a lid and usually a bail. The originals had no legs nor did they have a recessed lit but more often had a domed lid and were used for cooking at the hearth for most baking needs.

Later in the Colonial period, the new style of Dutch oven with legs was created. We often call it the camp Dutch oven. The legs make placing coals under the pot easier. You can place cooking coals on top of the lid for more even cooking and baking.

PICKING UP A NEW OR USED DUTCH OVEN

Finding a new Dutch oven is an easy enough task. Brands like Lodge have been making them in the U.S. since 1896. There are also many good brands of antique ovens from Wagner to Griswold, but many of these can be costly investments depending on rarity and size or type. My recommendation would be to buy a new one, as the investment is smaller until you find the style and size you like best. Once you have determined your preference, you can often find the more expensive versions at flea markets and sales and sometimes find a great deal on them as well.

Things to look out for are pits from rusting. Surface rust is easy to fix, but pits in the material are another story. When buying new, check to be sure the surfaces are smooth, especially on the inside, and there are no foundry blemishes. Check for even wall thickness throughout the sides of the pot as well as the lid rim if you are buying a camp-style oven.

If it has legs, ensure that these are not hollow legs that will gather dirt inside and eventually rust. Make sure it has a good, heavy bail and that the lid is a good fit. It should rotate easily on the oven but not have enough side-to-side movement that a gap can be seen.

PROS AND CONS OF ADDITIONAL COOKING EQUIPMENT

The main thing to remember is that all cooking gear is added weight, and that weight could be taken up by foodstuffs to prepare in case the hunting, fishing, or trapping does not go as planned. The more we can improvise, the better and the more compact the kit.

SKILLETS

Skillets are not a necessity unless you plan to fry or brown meat possibly to add to a larger dish like a stew or casserole.

Even then, meat can be browned quickly on a stick if need be (as long as it is not ground meat). Skillets do however come in very handy in a longer-term setup or when more folks are present and you plan to make fry breads or some type of fried grain meal like mush.

Now with all of that said, you can easily improvise a skillet or shallow pan from a stainless steel dish such as a dog bowl. It will fit well inside a bucket or pot, using pliers for a handle.

Some would say that it's easy enough to carry a skillet with a folding handle so it doesn't take up much room but it's all relative: A solid handle is likely to be more stable and so a better choice if you plan to carry a skillet at all. Again this comes down to an easy equation of weight versus rate. How much is carrying that weight going to do for me in the end and can I get by with something else to do the job like pliers and a dog bowl?

In the end, available conveyance will weigh heavily in decisions of this type. It makes no sense to pack a skillet unless you plan to use it and can afford the weight on your back.

REFLECTOR OVEN

One thing that you may consider worth the weight especially if traveling in a group is a reflector oven. These can be purchased or made from pie pans and are a great device that packs flat, weighs little, and is great for cooking anything from biscuits and breads to cookies and other desserts.

The basis of the reflector oven is just that it is used close to a burning fire to reflect heat from under and at the same time above a cook surface to provide even baking heat. These are ideal if you want some camp luxury. See Figure 7.2 for an example of a reflector oven in use.

EARTH OVENS

Also called rock or pit ovens, earth ovens are a simple way to cook food and have been around for thousands of years. Basically you dig a pit in the ground, lay a fire, place stones around it, then light the fire and let it burn to coals. The stones will absorb and radiate heat, so food placed in the pit will cook. Figure 7.3 shows an earth oven.

**Figure 7.2
Reflector oven**

**Figure 7.3
Earth oven**

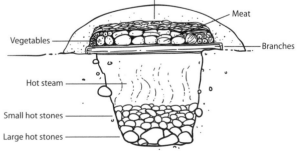

Layer of leaves and other moist material

Meat

Vegetables

Branches

Hot steam

Small hot stones

Large hot stones

CARRYING IN UTENSILS

If you plan to carry utensils in, they should be a match for the cookware you have. No, I don't mean like matching clothes; I mean a match to the material of the cook set for better results and less damage to patina and seasoning.

If you are using cast-iron or steel pots and pans, they will have a coating called a seasoning. If you use a metal utensil on this surface you chance removing and or scratching this causing food to stick. The same is true with nonstick pots and pans—the nonstick coating can easily be scratched. However, this is not a worry with stainless steel and aluminum pots and pans. Although aluminum will become scratched from steel utensils, softer metals won't hurt it. It is really common sense; you don't want a utensil harder than the cook surface, so match them to what's in your kit.

CARE FOR COOKWARE

To make your tools and utensils last longer, you have to take care of them. Here are my best tips for keeping your cookware in good shape.

WOODEN UTENSILS AND IMPLEMENTS

Wash clean using a very light abrasive (such as the rough scrubbing side of a sponge) if needed. Dry with a rag instead of letting them air-dry. Water left too long on wood can cause it to begin to rot. Once a month or so, rub a good coat of mineral oil into the wood with a soft cloth. This prevents the wood from drying out and splitting.

Wooden items made on the spot for use in camp that are not going to be taken out can be burned in the fire to dispose of them.

STAINLESS/ALUMINUM/TITANIUM METALS

These types of metal are fairly easily cared for. Wash as normal and allow to air-dry. Water used for cleaning should always be hot if possible. When soaps are not available, boil with water in the container over the fire before the final rinsing and scrubbing. If you need to scour the surface and do not have abrasives, fine sand from the creek bed will do. Just boil and rinse after this initial cleaning and allow to air-dry.

UNCOATED SHEET STEELS AND CAST IRON

These surfaces will be seasoned before and during use so avoid abrasives during cleanup. Scrape all remains of food from the surface with a wood scraper or a natural-material scrubbing brush. Boiling water in the container can loosen any stubborn foods left on the surface after cooking.

Once the surface is clean, wipe lightly with mineral oil on a rag. Do not let stand with water in the container for longer than a few hours if possible.

If rust appears on the surface, try to remove it without abrasives first. Implements like this that have rusted over time may require a soap-and-water scrubbing with an abrasive and re-seasoning of the surfaces for the cookware to be used again.

CLAY OR FIRED COOKWARE

If these containers have a glaze, they can be treated with care as a metal container for cleanup; they should be towel dried. If they are porous surfaces and unglazed, they will need to be seasoned and treated the same way as cast iron or sheet steel.

COOKING IRONS AND FIRE GEAR

Since these implements will get lots of abuse, being left in the rain within the fire pit and then charred by fire time and again, they will deteriorate over time if left unattended. As well they'll get everything black with soot if you don't clean them before storing. Between uses it does not hurt to heat them up and coat them with either a beeswax-and-turpentine mix or just paint them with a high-temperature black paint. They can be cleaned by wiping them down with a disposable rag and them oiled or waxed again to build a seasoning, or scrubbed and repainted between trips. The important thing is not to let rust build up on them over time.

TIPS AND TRICKS

- Companies like Palco made entire cook sets with nesting pots, pans, coffeepots, plates, and cups from the early 1900s. These sets can be had very inexpensively and can be broken down depending on your personal needs.
- Remember that items with multiple uses are better to carry than items that can only be used for one thing. An oven mitt is great for touching a hot pan, but that's all it does. A pair of thick leather gloves can serve as an oven mitt and also be used to clear brush around a campfire and other chores.
- When cleaning your cookware, liquid soaps and hot water can be used for everyday cleaning (don't use soap on cast iron) but avoid scrubbers made from any metal or hard abrasives.
- If your cast-iron cookware is new, food may stick to it a bit until it's seasoned. Use more oil or butter when cooking to help prevent sticking.
- To re-season cast iron, clean it thoroughly (using soap if you must), dry it completely, then coat it with cooking oil inside and out. Put it in a 400°F oven for 1 hour (place aluminum foil in the rack beneath it to catch any dripping oil). Turn off the oven and let the pan cool down inside the oven.

Chapter 8

TOOLS IMPROVISED FROM THE LANDSCAPE

"Learn to do common things uncommonly well; we must always keep in mind that anything that helps fill the dinner pail is valuable."

—George Washington Carver

If you have the time, you can construct almost any kind of utensil you will need for cooking, depending on available tools and your skill level. But sometimes a stick will do as good a job as anything; we tend to overthink things quite a bit. In a real tight spot, remember God gave you ten fingers for a reason.

CUTTING BOARDS AND PLANKS

The same piece of wood can be used for both carving food and for some cooking chores. A cutting board or cooking plank should be cut from a green hardwood, preferably one without resin, which will impart a bad taste to the food. The wood can be split from outside the pith of the tree trunk or large limb. It should be a minimum of about 4" wide by 12" long. You can create this using only a knife if the one you carry is capable of batoning without breaking (batoning is the process of splitting a piece of wood by driving a knife through it). An axe or larger chopping blade makes this an easy task.

You want this board to be about ½" thick when finished and smooth at least on the side that will be used. The flatter it is on both sides the more enjoyable and easier it will be to use.

Cedar, hickory, and maple make the best planks. Green wood is what you want for this application.

For grilling, you want the plank damp. Soaking it for an hour or so before use will accomplish this. For baking, the plank can be dry.

Plank grilling works best if the food and plank are enclosed in an oven setup. Any oven will work for this, be it earth, Dutch (if large enough), or reflector.

For baking, the plank is used merely as a platform that can be manipulated at an angle around the fire to cook things like bannocks or fish. The plank for grilling is placed directly on the rack or the floor of the oven to maximize heat, and the evaporating moisture will help keep the meat moist as it cooks; this works great for thinner steaks and fish.

UTENSILS

Depending on the task, a cleanly broken stick will work for lots of things. Carving one side of a small branch, about 2–3" wide, at an angle will work fine for a spatula for batter mixing and stew stirring. No need to be fancy with this. Again, green hardwood is preferred; use something with no resins to impart taste to the food.

Tongs are simple to create—cut a green sapling and carve a thin middle section on one side, then bend the branch in half to create the pinchers or tongs.

When I think about spoons, I figure they are nothing more than a shovel and don't need to be any fancier than that for a one-time use. Carve another 2" sapling and make a curved angular cut with your knife. Smooth it as best you can and call it good. If you live in an area with mussel shells, using a shell as a spoon is an easy solution. You can either hold it in your hand or lash it to a split green stick.

BUSHCRAFT TIP

Bark can make some handy tools fairly quick, from cups to spoons to ladles and simple trays for eating or for steam cooking.

CREATING NICER WOODEN UTENSILS

The creation of beautiful wood utensils for cooking and eating is a relaxing pleasure that's hard to match, but this should not be done at the time they are needed—if it's the last minute, then you use what is around you. If you desire to create nice utensils and keep them, there is time for this in camp or before the trip but some special tools will be needed in most cases for creating a concavity or "dishing out."

A good group of wooden utensils for a modest camp would be an eating spoon about tablespoon-sized and a larger serving spoon, a spatula, and a ladle. The ladle will take a bit more skill than the others but the more you make, the better you will become.

Create utensils from green wood. Remember that softer woods like poplar are easier and faster to carve but harder woods will last longer over time. In this book we will not get too deep into this subject as it could make a complete book alone, but there are a few simple rules to remember:

1. Don't use woods that have oils or resins within them. Coniferous trees have resin and should be avoided. Birch is an excellent choice as the oils are contained in the bark and it is a fine harder wood that carves nicely.
2. Avoid areas with knots or twisted grain.
3. Always remove the pith from the project piece.
4. The thinner you carve the piece, the less apt it is to crack while drying. This sounds counterintuitive, but wood shrinks as it dries, and the thicker it is while drying the more moisture is retained in some areas and less in others, which can cause the thick bowl of a spoon to crack as it dries.
5. Always work with the grain, not against. This will become obvious while carving, as working against the grain will remove chunks instead of fine slivers.

Start with a straight-grained branch or sapling about 4" in diameter. Cut a section about 12" long and split this in half with an axe or another tool. You will see the center pith when you split the piece. This should be removed by carving it off. You now have the blanks for two utensils, a serving spoon and a spatula. See Figure 8.1.

For the spatula, take one side and split off a veneer about ½" thick. You now have the leftover of that side to make an eating spoon. You should get three tools from one piece of wood easy enough.

There's no real trick in carving the basic shape for a flat spoon or for a spatula—it's a straightforward carving process. The basic carving can be done faster with a saw or an axe than a knife. Once the rough shape is made, then you are down to fine carving.

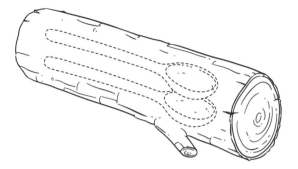

Figure 8.1 Serving spoon and spatula

Fashioning the bowl is the tedious part of the spoon process for the beginner, but with the right tool it goes very fast. Many would say at this point that a good spoon-carving knife or hook knife would be the tool for this, but for me the easiest to use and make short work of it is the gouge. A nice shallow sweep (or the depth of the concavity in the tool), about ¾–1" wide, will be plenty for any spoon bowl you wish to make. The same process can be used on ½ scale to make an eating spoon.

Spatulas are a bit easier with the same basic beginning steps. However, the end of the tool will be square or slightly angled and beveled over the length of the working end to make it chisel-like for getting under things in the pan. See Figure 8.2.

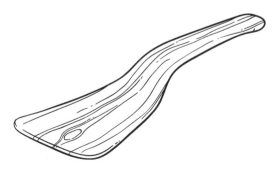

**Figure 8.2
Wooden spatula**

A simple whisk can be made by finding a sapling with several shoots growing from a central point. If this is cut at about 12" and the shoots cut to about 8" they can then be folded backward against the handle and lashed with cordage. See Figure 8.3.

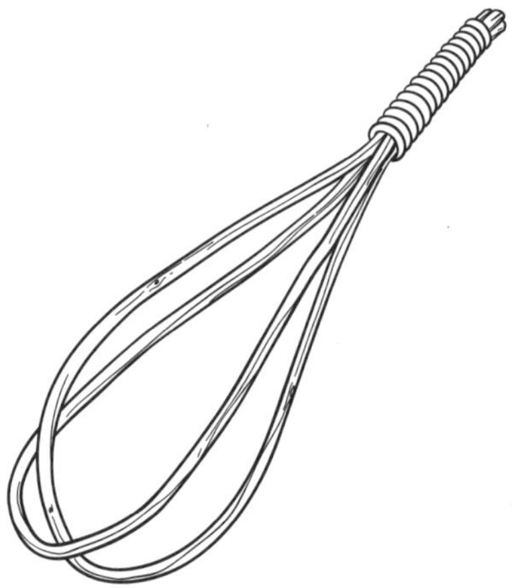

Figure 8.3 Wooden whisk

IMPROVISED CONTAINERS FROM THE LANDSCAPE

Containers are one of the hardest things to reproduce off the landscape. Making baskets and bark containers that are not watertight isn't too difficult, but containers you can actually cook in are a different matter. If you are in an area with stands of large-diameter bamboo, you have readymade containers of all types, but if not you are at the mercy of some more time-consuming and difficult methods, many of which will also dictate the way you can cook with them.

BURN-HOLLOWED CONTAINERS

Burning containers from wood is one of the oldest methods to make containers but also one of the most labor-intensive. It requires a good piece of green hardwood that is large enough to light a fire on, burn a controlled concavity into, and not leak after the fact. You can use a downfallen log for this provided it has no rot or insect damage that may compromise it after the burning process.

Once the wood is selected, place it on a flat surface. It may be necessary to split the log to create a flat area or hewn surface to work with. Build a small fire that is easy to control in the center of the wood. You will want to watch the sides closely and leave about 1" of thickness all around. You can slow the process on the edges by adding wet mud or clay as you go. After it starts to burn, remove the coals and scrape the burnt area to the bare wood, creating a concavity. Then add coals to the fresh scraped wood and begin the burn process again. A tube to blow on the coals and direct air for more heat in some areas will help with control as well.

BARK CONTAINERS

Barks are a great container-making resource, especially if the containers do not have to be watertight. However, with the proper materials and a bit more effort, they can also be made watertight. The simplest way to construct a bark container is with folded birch bark, but other barks like poplar work well, especially in the spring when the sap is running and they are easily removed from the tree.

Bark-lashed containers are easily made from poplar barks in the spring. To remove these barks from the tree it is necessary to split the bark on the tree the length of the container doubled plus an additional amount for the bottom, depending on the size of the container being made. Pick an area of the trunk at least half again the diameter of the finished desired container, to allow for shrinkage when drying, and try to pick an area with no knots or branches.

Split the bark vertically this length and then slip your knife or axe blade under the bark to lift it away from the tree. You can construct a quick spud for prying the bark from any green branch by cutting a single-sided wedge on the end of a 1–2" branch. This will aid in lifting larger pieces away from the tree. Once the bark is removed in one sheet, it can be scored and folded, then punched and laced with inner bark cordage or any cordage you have available.

Be sure to also punch a row of holes around the top and lace an additional piece of split material around the rim for stability and add a handle as you wish from a bent green branch or another split or riving.

TIPS AND TRICKS

- As with utensils you pack in, think about how you can use a tool you make for more than one application to save effort and resources.
- Tools that you've made from the environment can be burned in a campfire if you do not plan to pack them out with you.
- Use the fibrous material from the inner bark of a tree as cordage for making utensils.
- Use your imagination. Look around you and use what's already in the natural environment. A turtle shell could be used as a container (boil the shell before using). A square log could be cut and hollowed out for a cooking pot. Leaves could be used to wrap food for cooking (in place of aluminum foil).
- Tools and utensils you make from the environment are throwaway items (or add-to-the-fire items) as with most quickly improvised tools, so cleaning and sterilizing are truly not an issue, although a good soaking in a boiling kettle will take care of this for a next-day use.

— Chapter 9 —
QUICK BUSH TOOLS

"In wildness is the preservation of the world."
—Henry David Thoreau

Many quick tools and apparatus can be fashioned from wood if you understand simple notches, knots, and lashings. Many hooks and suspension devices can be used for holding a pot above a fire from a crossbar, galley pole, or tripod. Simple toggles are amazing tools and very versatile in camp cooking as well. Quick gambrels (a bar for hanging carcasses) can be made for aid in skinning game, and simple cooking devices as well as ovens can be fashioned from wood and stone.

POT CRANE

To hang a pot, you can create a makeshift pot crane by taking a strong green sapling and laying it at an angle to a rock or log, and driving one end into the ground. Notch the other end to hold the pot over the fire. This will suffice for any one-pot meal. See Figure 9.1.

Figure 9.1 Pot crane

GALLEY POLE AND ROTISSERIE

A simple galley pole and rotisserie are easy to make. Cut two green, forked saplings to the same length, about 3–4' long. Hammer the non-forked end of each post into the ground on opposite sides of the fire pit. Use a simple crossbar made from another sapling to hang a pot over the fire. You can use a couple of notched hooks (metal ones if you prefer) to adjust the height of the pot.

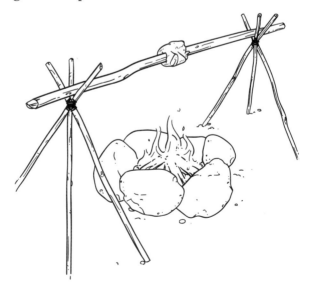

Figure 9.2 Improvised rotisserie

When choosing forked wood, do not use Y-shaped branches, as these will normally split when pounded. Instead use a fork that is caused by a branch growing out at an angle from the tree or larger branch.

If a rotisserie (a spit that turns) is needed, find another fork. This one can be an actual Y branch that is green and long enough to reach both upright posts. See Figure 9.2.

TRIPODS

Tripods are one of the most useful items one can fashion and can be adapted to create many ways of cooking in camp. Saplings of green hardwood will serve best. Take three similar-sized saplings and lash them together. These can be lashed with a tripod lash, or a simple metal ring can be carried to make things even simpler. See Figure 9.3.

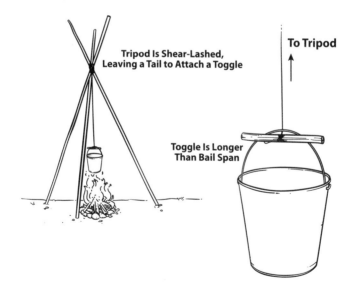

Figure 9.3 Cooking tripod

THE CANTERBURY CAMP CITCHEN

A camp kitchen can be built easily enough from a tripod structure. You can make it as simple as a hanging pot over the fire or as elaborate as a smoking rack or roasting grid. To build the multifunctional kitchen setup that I have coined the Canterbury Camp Citchen, we start with a basic tripod. Then add three short forks lashed about mid-height, one to each leg. The last fork at the apex of the triangle should be lashed facing inward with the other two to the outside. Add three sticks for cross members that can be easily removed when not being used.

On the front or open side of the tripod, the cross-stick should be a bit longer than the other two so that utensils can be hung out of the way of the cooking but handy when needed. If a rack is needed you can now cut and notch simple cross members to fill in this triangle. These also can be removed when not in use.

From the center of the tripod, build an adjustable trammel (hook mechanism) of cord and a notched stick. You can add or remove this depending on the cooking style for that meal. Several hooks should be created for the longest cross-stick for hanging more than one cooking container over the fire as well.

The utility of a tripod cannot be overstated as it is easily adjusted both in span and axis to adjust things over and closer or farther away from the fire using a trammel or hooks for micro adjustments. See Figure 9.4 for a closer look at the adjustable trammel.

If you want to use this for baking or smoking, an emergency space blanket wrapped around the outside of the tripod, reflective side in, works a treat.

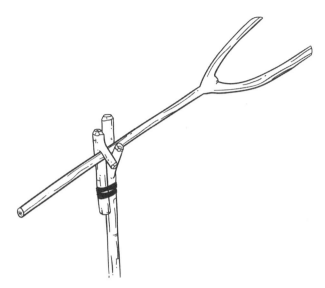

Figure 9.4 Adjustable trammel

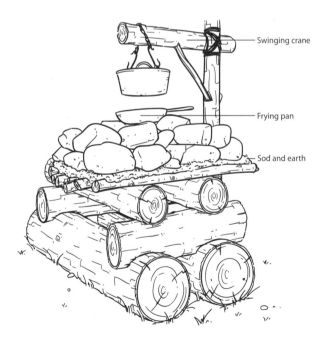

Swinging crane

Frying pan

Sod and earth

Figure 9.5 Altar kitchen

RAISED HEARTH

If you desire a more permanent solution that can be very comfortable to cook on and works well in areas of fire danger you can build a fire altar or raised hearth. This is accomplished with natural materials by building a log box about 40" high and rectangular in shape about 3' × 4'. Fill the inside with dirt and build the fire on the top. Forks and uprights with galley poles can be added for hanging pots over the fire as well. This makes for a comfortable cook setup, and things like clay ovens can be built to one side easy enough for long-term use. See Figure 9.5.

OTHER FIELD EXPEDIENT CONTAINERS AND COOK POTS

It is fairly easy to make a cook set from simple food cans after they are emptied. You can make a cooking pot just by using a can opener! A #10 can (such as a coffee can) makes a great cook pot especially if a bail is added made from bailing or trapping wire. See Figure 9.6.

You can fashion a cup out of a smaller soup-sized can. A plastic soda bottle will fit inside this for a canteen. A heavier Gatorade-type bottle can fit in a slightly larger stew can. You can wrap wire around the smaller can to create a handle and punch holes in the #10 for a bail wire. If you add a stew can with a tuna can upside down, you have a lid for a smaller pot as well, and if you feel the need for a skillet, a dollar-store pie pan will suffice well. Use a pair of cheap pliers as a handle. This skillet can double as a plate.

A folded sheet of heavy tinfoil for roasting envelopes would round this out nicely for easy cooking on a budget or for a school project.

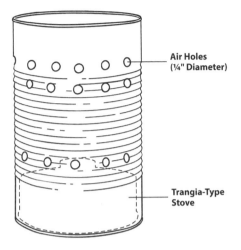

Figure 9.6 Tin can cookware

OTHER UNCONVENTIONAL COOKWARE

There are lots of things we can use to cook with that we don't consider most of the time. Dog bowls, for example, can be found in a variety of sizes and depths in stainless steel and are very inexpensive. These make great pans when coupled with pliers for a handle. Two of these stacked opposite and connected with metal binder clips make a great little baker, and since they nest inside each other that makes it an easy carry for sure.

Gold pans (which have deep sides) are still available in steel. They also make good skillets and plates and become multi-functional depending on your activity in the outdoors. I have cooked everything in a gold pan from fish to baked beans.

Hubcaps, in an emergency, can be used for boiling water or cooking once they are cleaned out well, provided they are metal.

CLAY OVEN

To make a clay oven you need some decent clay that is fairly clean. Good places to look for this are around creek banks in many parts of the eastern woodlands. Collect a couple of 5-gallon buckets full of clay and take them back to camp. If you want to make pots or vessels for cooking, the clay will need to be cleaned and then mixed with a binder like cattail fluff or sand. If you are making an oven, you can pretty much use it as is.

BUSHCRAFT TIP

You can also use clay to cook small mammals, fish, and birds. Gut the game item first and cut off head and feet. There is no need to skin or pluck it. Instead of wrapping it in foil, mold clay around the game completely (no scales, fur, or feathers should show). Then place it in the coals to cook. When the clay hardens, break it and pull it away from the game item. (Cooking time varies, but expect it to take an hour or so.) Feathers, scales, fur, and other inedible parts come away with the clay.

On a flat surface, build up a mound of damp soil the size you want the inside of the oven to be, then cover this with clay about ½" thick all the way around the dome. In an hour or so on a good sunny day the clay will be hard enough so you can carve and remove an opening in the front and a chimney or draft hole in the top about 2–4" in diameter.

Leave the rest to dry in the sun a couple of days until the exterior feels hard, then carefully dig out the dirt from the inside and build a small fire within the oven. Gradually build the fire up to fire the inside of the oven. If all goes well, you can cook in the oven by spreading hot coals to the side and placing food to cook in the center. See Figure 9.7.

Figure 9.7 Clay oven

ITEMS NEEDED TO PROCESS FOOD

We've discussed the equipment you will need for cooking and eating your meals but we haven't yet discussed the tools you will need to process the food. We must always consider cutting tools that will be needed for the task since these are less likely to be something you can just knock together on the spot. You want to consider bringing or packing them in.

- **Knife:** You will undoubtedly have some type of knife with you. I always prefer a butchering-style blade for a sheath knife. If you have a good stout belt knife, you have an advantage for processing food.
- **Ulu knife:** Another good tool to throw in the pack is the hash knife or ulu. The curved blade on this knife comes in

real handy for everything from dicing veggies to skinning game. They are usually lightweight as well.

- **Axe or hatchet:** Your axe or hatchet, as well as the saw you carry, can help with big-game processing.
- **Saw:** Many folding bucksaws have options of a bone-cutting blade, but a hacksaw will work fine. A 12" tubular bucksaw works well for processing wood and is easy to get hacksaw blades to fit, making it a more versatile tool around camp. Bahco makes a 12" saw that can be purchased with both a green wood and hacksaw blade in one package. The best thing about tubular frames is they are near indestructible if you can pack them in.
- **Pliers:** A good pair of old fencing pliers is most always in my kit. They can be used to skin a catfish, strip the tailbone from an animal, or lift a pot lid from a Dutch oven. They also make something great for grabbing the bail of a hot pot when removing it from the fire and carrying it to where food is served.
- **Measuring tools:** A couple of measuring devices will help and can be improvised by marking measurements on your camp cup and making your eating spoon about a tablespoon in size.

METAL COOKING APPARATUS

If you have a permanent camp or have conveyance, you may choose to carry metal or forged cooking apparatus. If you are packing fairly light, you can still carry some steel. Some of these items can save aggravation and time, making camp life more enjoyable as well.

FIRE IRONS

While two green logs of similar diameter make a fine temporary placement for pots and pans with a fire built between, fire irons make life much more tolerable and weigh only 2 pounds. These are flat irons made from metal stock about 1.5" wide and 24" long. They can be placed on logs or rocks with fire underneath and are adjustable to accommodate different pans and pots. Because they are flat steel they are long-lasting and easy enough to straighten in case they get bent. See Figure 9.8.

Figure 9.8 Fire irons

CHAINS AND TRAMMELS

One thing that can make life much easier and make you feel safer in the long run if you don't have as much experience with carving wood implements is to carry a light chain with a hook on each end, running about 18–24" long. This can serve the function of adjusting pots over the fire whether from a tripod or a galley pole.

Trammels are another item that make small adjustments possible. You can easily fashion them with light chain and a straight rod bent at 90° on the top ½". Shape a hook to hold a pot on the bottom. The hook can be slid up the chain through the bottom link and then hooked at various intervals in the hanging chain to adjust at one-link increments the length of the trammel.

TIPS AND TRICKS

- Utensils and tools need be nothing more than from the kitchen drawer or a Goodwill shop and can be had for very little. These can be heated in the fire and bent for packability if necessary.
- Forged cook systems can be made or bought depending how handy you are and whether you have the necessary equipment. You can buy these at various wilderness outfitters.
- Skewer cooking doesn't have to be fancy. If you can shove a sharp stick into it and hold it over the fire, there's no need for complicated equipment.
- Cooking irons can still be found secondhand and can be used to make hot sandwiches, pies, and other treats.
- Tripods can be used to increase the amount of cooking area you have. One dish can be cooking suspended from the tripod while another cooks in a skillet or in a foil-wrapped packet on the coals below.
- Tripods can also be used for other camp chores. A rope strung between two tripods makes a handy clothesline.

— Chapter 10 —
TYPES OF COOKING

"Cookery means . . . English thoroughness, French art, and Arabian hospitality; it means the knowledge of all fruits and herbs and balms and spices; it means carefulness, inventiveness, and watchfulness."

—JOHN RUSKIN

There are several ways of cooking over a fire. Each method means the food and fire are manipulated differently. In this chapter, we'll cover the most common methods of camp cooking and show you how to prepare tasty meals no matter which approach you take.

FRYING

In frying food we do not want any flames or even large coals. They can interfere with the evenness of the heat or cause the food to burn. You should rake a thin bed of coals away from the fire so that a skillet can be placed directly on top of it. If you're planning for a quick meal, then an initial fire of only kindling-sized sticks will provide this fairly fast. With the initial flames, you can heat water for coffee if you wish.

Too much heat will burn grease or fat, giving the meat a nasty aftertaste, so be careful not to cook directly over the hottest part of the fire.

If you have an excess of grease or lard you can fry directly in a pool of it. Just heat it to the point it begins to bubble, then place small pieces of meat directly in the grease, turning them over once to complete the frying process. You can remove these from the grease and place on anything absorbent to soak up excess grease before serving hot.

If you are traveling with limited grease you can heat the pan on the coals and fry the fattiest portions first. If this is not an option, use just enough of the grease that you do have to keep the meat from sticking to the pan and proceed.

Remember that any fat or grease used for frying fish should not be used for any other foods or it will give it a fishy flavor for sure. Small game is best cooked by cutting it into small pieces and frying, then serving with a gravy mix that can easily be carried in packets.

BROILING

For broiling meat we want to sear it first to lock in the juices. This means placing the meat momentarily in open flame to quickly dry the outside and create an insulating skin over the inner meat.

SPIT BROILING

Broiling should be done just on the edge of a bed of hot coals on a stick, spit, or cooking fork. Cut the meat approximately 1" thick. You want to be able to catch any dripping to baste the meat while cooking so some type of catchment will be needed. It should only take about 5 minutes to broil a steak this size. Serve with drippings and melted butter. Don't season till you're finished cooking.

A fowl can be split in two pieces or just split open for broiling. Fish can be cut open and broiled on a green wood frame.

PAN BROILING

Broiling can be done in a shallow, covered pan if the meat is turned often.

ROCK BROILING

If you have to broil on rocks, take two flat rocks, clean of debris, that are not from near a creek or moist in any way (moist or wet rocks may explode when heated). Place them one on top of another in the coals with a series of rocks between to form an oven. Build the fire up to heat the rocks, then wipe away any debris after it burns to coals again and cook meat between the rocks. Another option is to suspend an old auto rim or grill grate off the ground with a few rocks.

All these things can provide a solid cooking surface as well as containing the heat. As with any cook oven, the goal is to contain the heat and keep it on the food to be cooked. See Figure 10.1.

**Figure 10.1
Rock oven**

ROASTING

You roast meat by placing it in the direct heat of the fire. Do this by placing meat above a good hot coal bed on a spit or fork. Roasting works best with a fire backing of some sort, whether it be rocks or logs to help direct heat back by thermal mass onto the cooking meat.

As with other forms of cooking, always sear the meat over open flame first to lock in flavor. Meat being roasted on a spit should be turned in ¼-turn increments. Meat and fowl can also be suspended with a stout cord. A paddle added to the string will turn the meat slowly with the rising heat from the fire.

Gravy goes well with roasted meats. You can also roast meat in a reflector oven before the fire. The meat should be basted with its own juices as it cooks.

BRAISING

Braising is the best thing for tough cuts of meat and is a bit between frying and baking. Place about 2" or so of water in a shallow pan that can be covered. Add some fresh vegetables, like onion and maybe a clove of garlic, then add the meat, cover, and cook over coals about 15 minutes to the pound. About 20–30 minutes before the meat is finished, add seasonings like Old Bay or seasonings of your choice.

BAKING

Baking is generally done in a sealed container of some sort. There are many ways of doing this, and it allows for the addition of other ingredients including liquids, like water, wine, liquors, or other types of marinades as well. The main thing about baking that differs from other methods is really producing a fairly even amount of heat surrounding what is being cooked. This is easily accomplished by cooking in a Dutch oven, baker, or in an envelope of aluminum foil. Cast-iron cookware helps evenly distribute heat, so it is a good choice for baking.

BOILING

When boiling, you'll need a good pot or bucket. The wider and shorter the pot, the faster it will boil due to surface area above the fire, but a bucket will do as well. The best thing, I find, is to paint metal cookware black with high-temperature paint. I do this before going to the field. The metal will heat up faster this way when fuel is a resource to be conserved.

Add fresh meat to already boiling water; meat for stews should be started in the water when it is cold so it will heat up more slowly, releasing its flavor to the water.

Boil meat until it falls free of the bone, and it should be good and done. If you have vinegar a few tablespoons will help tenderize meat. Season boiled meat a few minutes before it is done. If you are going to eat fresh meat, add it to a rolling boil for 5 minutes or so to lock in the juices and then remove it and cook it above the fire as normal.

If you desire a thicker soup, you may simmer it after cooking for about 30 minutes and add some instant potatoes or JAW biscuit mix and stir often as it simmers.

STEWING

Stewing is the slowest process of cooking and should be reserved for the toughest cuts and types of meat. Coyote is a good stewing candidate as the meat is fairly tough even in the best cuts. Use lean meats only for stewing and again lock flavor in by browning quickly or boiling for 5 minutes.

Reduce water to approximately a pint or so for one person. Add a soup stock if you have it or some bullion, add a couple of ounces of flour as a thickener, and bring the contents to a boil. Add some salt, pepper, and or curry powder, depending on your taste. Old Bay works great here (use about 1 tablespoon per serving). Then cover the pot and simmer 4–5 hours. You can add potatoes to thicken the stew as well, and dried soup greens make an excellent addition to the pot as well before simmering.

STEAMING

Steaming is cooking with hot moisture, and works well for vegetables as well as fish. This is best accomplished with a steamer if you have one but can also be done with a campfire. To accomplish this, place several dry stones in your campfire to get them red-hot. Dig a hole large enough for the stones to fit inside along with food, leaving enough space around them for insulation. Locate the steaming chamber somewhere proximal to the fire.

Place the heated stones in the hole and cover them with a thin layer of wet grass or leaves, then place food on top of this followed by more wet leaves and grass. Fill the hole with loose earth and poke a hole in the top down to food level. Pour some water into the hole and immediately plug the hole to stop the release of steam and hold it within the chamber created to steam the food.

TIPS AND TRICKS

- For baking, using a small pot (with the food to be baked) within a larger pot helps ensure even heating. Cover the larger pot with aluminum foil or a lid to help retain heat.

Put a small amount of water in the larger pot to create steam for a crustier texture, such as when baking bread.

- When cooking in a Dutch oven (particularly baking), put coals beneath and on top of the oven.
- When cooking on a wood fire, remember that you need different kinds of heat for different kinds of food. Water can be boiled over a high flame, and stews can be cooked over a low flame; most other foods are cooked over coals. Coals hot enough to cook over look grayish white.
- A lightweight grill can be a useful piece of equipment; grill directly on it or use it as a platform for a pot to boil or steam.
- All camp cooking should be done outdoors, regardless of the exact fuel and setup you're using. Make sure the area around and above your cooking area is clear of debris, shrubbery, and any plant matter.

PART 3
Living Off the Land

CLOVER

CATTAIL

SORREL

EDIBLE

SAFE PLANTS

EDIBLE

SAFE PLANTS

VIOLET

PLANTAIN

WILD ONION

EDIBLE

DANDELION

ONION GARLIC

RASPBERRIES

SAFE PLANTS

EDIBLE

SAFE PLANTS

BLACK WALNUT

WINTERCRESS

RAMPS

EDIBLE

BURDOCK

ACORN

PURSLANE

HICKORY NUT

SAFE PLANTS

AVOID

LOOK-ALIKE PLANTS

MILKWEED

QUEEN ANNE'S LACE

DOGBANE

HEMLOCK

AVOID

POISONOUS PLANTS

MAYAPPLE

POKEWEED

— Chapter 11 —

HUNTING AND TRAPPING GAME: FUNDAMENTALS

"Man is the only animal that can remain on friendly terms with the victims he intends to eat until he eats them."

—SAMUEL BUTLER

This topic could take up an entire volume in and of its own! But in this chapter, I am going to cover the basics that will give the most success while hunting and trapping in primitive fashion. For our purposes, we're looking to hunt and trap edible food; we're not trying to trap for fur or anything like that.

LOCATING ANIMALS

Hunting is a skill set all its own, and to be a good trapper one must be a good hunter as well—not in the sense of being able to catch prey necessarily, although that is the end game, but knowing where the game will likely be at a given time. This is the key to success in both skills; the rest will come in time.

For both hunting and trapping there are legalities to follow: licenses, tags, method of take, and size or type of animal and even sex in some cases. Once you are armed with the proper permissions, you can begin hunting. The first thing to learn is where to go to find your prey, no matter your chosen method of dispatching the animal.

Animals have many things in common with people. They need water, food, and shelter or cover that protects them from both severe weather and predators. Understanding your prey will help solve the puzzle of finding then.

GAME TRAILS

If an animal like a squirrel is known to prefer hickory nuts, then the most obvious place to find a squirrel is in an area with lots of these trees around. All animals will need water, so any location that has a single water source such as a small pond is a great place to look. If crop fields are near your location, this will feed many animals like raccoons and deer, and these are a good place to start. Any open field with low-growing browse forage is a good place to find deer and rabbits.

Animals prefer to travel in certain ways and at certain times. Understanding this will help you key in to areas for hunting and ambush as well know when travel routes can be found between the areas mentioned previously. Most animals travel the same game trails daily. They prefer the path of least resistance. Some animals prefer higher ground; for instance, minks and raccoons will travel along bank lines to forage for food, but a deer is more likely to travel down from higher ground and then pretty much straight back up from a creek or stream. These are all animal behavioral clues that a wise hunter understands.

IMPACT OF WEATHER

Weather has an effect on animal movement. A front like rain or cold will cause animals to move. Moon phases have a great effect on salt-water fishing and maybe some effect on shallow-water fishing, especially on full moonlit nights. Fish in shallow water see movement from above. Even just the shadow of movement can trigger a flight response, so full moonlit nights have to be treated as sunny days and some stealth may be necessary on such nights to catch fish in shallow water. But moon phases are not the major determining factor in upland game movement.

BUSHCRAFT TIP

Spot-and-stalk hunting is a slow methodical process. Oftentimes you take a few steps an hour, depending on the situation. Still, hunting will usually be from an ambush point like a known travel route, where you'll wait for the game to come to you. Understanding the animals' behavior will aid in both instances.

Temperature however does have great effect on movements of animals, especially during the hunting seasons, generally fall and winter. For a long time, many hunters have believed that the day before, day of, and day after a full moon are times when deer do not move. However, this is greatly dependent on temperatures. If it is unseasonably warm on these days, then the old tales hold true and upland animals tend to not move but on cold fronts they seem to move no matter the moon phase.

ANIMAL BEHAVIOR

To be effective hunters and trappers, we must understand that all animals need the same things we do: shelter, water, and food. If we understand the routes animals use to obtain and move from one to the other, we can recognize good places for hunting and trapping them. Useful information to have is a working knowledge of what the target animals eat, where they live, and where they travel.

Animals are predictable to a certain degree, and understanding the patterns of their movements will also help us increase numbers of animals caught or spotted, whether we are trapping with primitive or modern traps or hunting or a combination of all of these.

Beyond requiring shelter, water, and food, an animal's sole purpose in life is reproduction of its species. Animals are most relaxed when sleeping, followed by traveling to and from a feeding or watering area. They are most wary when feeding or watering. Remember that animals will travel on the same routes most of the time depending on season, and they can be patterned because of this.

But because of this, they, like you, can recognize when something has changed in their direct environment. While scent of humans is nothing new to an animal, changes like a trap set in the area may take a couple passes to overwhelm the curiosity. So be prepared to wait it out, and don't get anxious because a trap has not been visited or tampered with in 48–72 hours after it is set.

ANIMAL SIGN

Animal sign is the key to successful hunting and trapping. Do not waste your time hunting or trapping where there is no sign.

Sign is anything the animal leaves that is a trace that it passed through the area. Because animal behavior is somewhat predictable, if an animal has passed through a certain area, it is likely he will pass again.

There are seven types of sign we need to be familiar with and this familiarity will help us identify things like species, eating habits, and numbers.

1. **Tracks**. Tracks of an animal are the easiest way to identify species and can also help with numbers and frequency of travel in that area. See Figure 11.1.

Figure 11.1 Animal tracks

2. **Scat.** Scat left when the animal defecates can identify species as well as what the animal is currently foraging on.
3. **Slough.** Slough is something from the animal's body left behind after it is gone. It could be hair left on a fence wire, a feather dropped while preening, or the shed skin from a snake.
4. **Remains.** Remains is the carcass of an animal. This will not only provide bait for other traps but also may give some idea of other animals like coyotes or foxes in the area. Obviously, if there is one that is dead there are surely more as well.
5. **Refuse.** Refuse is the animal's garbage, what it has left after feeding, that will help identify its species and its travel routes. Refuse may be a squirrel's midden (areas where they have eaten lots of nuts or are digging and eating stored nuts; it will be littered with shells), or it could be the chewed trees and branches left by beaver or muskrat.
6. **Dens.** Dens are the animal's home: holes in the ground, in the bank, or in the hollow of a tree. Many times we can tell species from this sign alone.
7. **Odor.** Odor is the trickiest. Cat urine has a distinct smell; so too does the smell of rotten meat from a carnivore den, like that of a fox. Obviously you would smell a skunk in the area, but you can identify other subtle smells as well.

TIPS AND TRICKS

- The early morning and late afternoon will often yield the better results when hunting and trapping.
- You can use bait animals to lure food animals. These bait animals are the animals that every other animal seeks as its food. Animals found in or around the water's edge fit this

category very well—think frogs, crayfish, and fish, as well as mussels and snails.

- Knowing what the target animal eats is another important factor in success in trapping because a baited trap is about a hundred times more likely to catch an animal than a not-baited set.

- All states require hunters to take hunter-training classes, so don't be surprised if you're asked to show proof that you've fulfilled this requirement before you're allowed the necessary hunting licenses and permits.

- If you haven't hunted or trapped before, think small. Keep your expectations to a minimum, and don't think you need to buy every possible gear item to succeed.

Chapter 12

HUNTING: BEYOND THE BASICS

"For us, hunting wasn't a sport. It was a way to be intimate with nature, that intimacy providing us with wild, unprocessed food, free from pesticides and hormones, and with the bonus of having been produced without the addition of great quantities of fossil fuel. In addition, hunting provided us with an ever-scarcer relationship in a world of cities, factory farms, and agribusiness—direct responsibility for taking the lives that sustained us, lives that even vegans indirectly take as the growing and harvesting of organic produce kills deer, birds, snakes, rodents, and insects. We lived close to the animals we ate, we knew their habits, and that knowledge deepened our thanks to them and the land that made them."

—TED KERASOTE,

MERLE'S DOOR: LESSONS FROM A FREETHINKING DOG

When it comes to hunting for small and medium game, nothing can match the versatility of the shotgun. There are lots of choices out there, so understanding a bit about the true possibilities will help you decide. I have settled on a single-shot break-open gun as my choice for many reasons I hope to explain here.

GUN CONSIDERATIONS

Two huge factors in choosing a weapon for hunting are weight and simplicity of its mechanisms. Weight matters if you'll be carrying the weapon for long periods, and simplicity of mechanism means fewer problems are likely to occur and maintenance is easier to do.

One thing we need to look at for versatility's sake is the age of the gun as well as the chamber length and choke. The choke is a reduction in the barrel's outside diameter that allows the gun to pattern better at distance but does give some restriction on loads, especially hand loads and muzzle loads.

GUN AGE

First to the age of the gun: You want something modern enough that it was made to withstand the use of modern powders, not just black powder charges. You also want a good quality steel barrel. Most guns made after 1940 will meet this restriction, and you will be fine with any gun made in the past 50 years that is in sound working order.

CHAMBER LENGTH

Next you want to look at chamber length. This is the area in which the shell is loaded at the breech. You want this to be a 3" chamber so it will accept any load you can find or buy to put in the gun. Many modern shells are 3", and if you have a 2¾" chamber, such shells will be useless without modification.

CHOKE

The basic chokes are cylinder, modified, and full. They get progressively smaller from cylinder to full, with modified being the happy medium. Cylinder bore is fine but you will sacrifice accuracy past 20–25 yards for sure, while modified will keep a good pattern with a modern shell to about 35 yards. Again the tradeoff for choke is load variation and adaptability.

BUSHCRAFT TIP

My main carry gun is an H&R single-shot 12-gauge shotgun with a modified choke and a 26" barrel. I find this to be the perfect gun for running the woods.

BARREL LENGTH

Barrel length is a matter of personal preference, but I find that anything over 24" is as accurate as 30". Most shots we will take with these guns are short-yardage shots anyway, and added barrel length is added weight.

ROUNDS

Let's first speak of store-bought modern rounds and the versatility of that beautiful old SS 12GA. I have a great deal of variation in loads and game I can hunt with this gun with little or no modification to anything

- #8 shot for small birds
- #6 shot for small game
- #4 shot for large waterfowl and turkey
- Slugs or buckshot for larger game

Just this gives me a huge array of animals I can hunt by only carrying a few shells and the gun if I am determined to make my supper from hunted game.

SUBCALIBER ADAPTERS

Now let's explore a bit more of the modified versatility of this gun beyond normal 12GA store-bought ammo. Subcaliber adapters come in many different types. First let's look at shotgun calibers. I can buy adapters that are 3" for my chamber to accept 20GA and 410GA, as well as with that adapter 45 Long Colt pistol cartridges. Now I can shoot any type 20 or 410GA shell as well as any 12GA shell in any chamber length up to 3".

There are also 8" adapters that are 3" chambers and rifled to shoot most pistol cartridges including 9mm, 38, 40, and 45ACP, as well as rifle cartridges in 22LR (long rifle), 22WMR (Winchester Magnum Rimfire), and 17HMR (Hornady Magnum Rimfire).

Now I have a whole other realm of possibilities for my lil 12GA, and I can easily match my sidearm to the gun for safety if one fails. The rifled adapters are surprisingly accurate especially at 30 yards or less, again normal small game ranges. The 20GA, 410, and a 3" rifled 22 also come in what's called a "stack pack" that all fit into each other like a nesting cook set and can be carried in a small waterproof container, taking up little room in the kit.

RELOADING SPENT SHELLS

You don't have to purchase tools to reload a shell in the field. What you may already have will work. First, we need to cut the old crimp from the shell, and our knife will do the job fine. Cut the crimp so that the shell is 3" total length for the chamber. Then we need to remove the spent 209 primer from the shell before seating a new one.

REPLACING THE PRIMER

Removing the old primer requires an anvil to create space where the old primer can be pressed out. Several washers glued together will work for this or just a hardwood board with about a ⅜" hole drilled into it works fine. Make this anvil (whether of washers or wood) about ½" thick to ensure the primer completely clears the shell when removed. I use a simple piece of scrap metal about ½" thick by 2" × 3" for this tool, and it works well in the next step to seat the new primer as well.

Place the shell on the anvil with the spent primer over the hole in the anvil, and use a normal flat punch or a ground-down 20-penny nail to drive the old primer out from the inside of the shell with a light blow from a mallet or hammer. Once the old primer is out, inspect the shell to ensure there are no cracks in either the brass or the plastic (if using a high-brass cartridge).

To seat the new primer, we need a box of 209 SG primers. These are readily available and come in packs of 100. Seat the primer the best you can by hand pressure ensuring the alignment is even going into the primer pocket. Now place the shell primer down on the flat metal surface of the anvil (a solid flat surface like metal is important). Take a common 5⁄16" deep well socket and a short adapter and place this over the primer pocket on the inside of the shell and again tap until the new primer seats. Simple enough. You now have a primed shell ready to load again.

RELOADING THE SHELL

To load the shell we need powder (black or Pyrodex). The beauty of Pyrodex is overloading or overcharging is much harder, and Pyrodex powders are Walmart shelf items at about $12–$15 a pound. This should load 65–80 shells, depending on your load.

We will also need some wad and over wad/over shot carding. The wad can be any soft material. In the field, I prefer to use sheep's wool from my trapping supply kit, as it is somewhat lubricating as well as fire retardant after leaving the barrel of the gun.

To make our over wad/over shot carding we need a cutter. This cutter can be made from sharpened tube stock of steel with a ⅝" ID. Bevel the outer edges to create the cutting edge, then use this with a mallet to cut cardboard stock cards in circles.

Once we have these supplies we need to have a measure for powder and shot. This can be made from tubing as well. Mine is copper with one end smashed and a hole drilled for a lanyard. I can use this for both reloading and muzzle loading.

This measure should hold a particular volume of powder. About 60 grains is standard for the 12GA, and you can use this for an equal volume of shot.

The final step is using a glue gun to seal the top of the shell once loaded.

TALKING SHOT

Let's talk about shot for a moment. Remember we are measuring shot in volume, so the amount will vary with size. You can buy lead shot in bulk. The best all-round size for functional use is #6 shot, as it will kill birds, most small game, and will take medium animals as well, especially at close range.

The other kind of shot that is worth a look is actual BBs. They are very inexpensive as well as versatile and will be useful for about all game except small fowl. The only issue to remember with steel BBs is they cannot be melted down easily to make round ball or slugs.

LOADING THE SHOT

There is an easy sequence to be used here every time to make a good shell. Set the primed cartridge on end and load a measure of powder, then a wad of wool (this amount will need to be figured as you make shells due to compression; the material is not easily measured for volume). Add an over wad card (cardboard cutout), then a volume of shot.

The final piece to add is an over shot card. At this point the shell should be filled to the top of where it was cut off (this is an adjustment to wad that you will always have to make when reloading a spent shell).

You can now seal the rim of the shell with hot glue to keep the contents in the shell, and you have a usable shotgun shell. Less is more on the hot glue; an electric melting gun makes the job easier than using a lighter to melt the glue stick, although the lighter will work in the field.

ROUND BALL

Let's speak of round balls for a moment. If we are using a modified choke gun, it will have an ID at the end of the barrel. If it is approximately .071" or 71 caliber, I would suggest getting a lead ball mold of about .069". This will allow for a good, thick patch when muzzle loading and allow for wall thickness of the cartridge when reloading.

Shot is very difficult to reproduce, while round balls are easy. You will use much more shot for hunting than you will round balls, so carrying shot in volume and making a few round balls as needed makes more sense.

MUZZLE LOADING

Now let's look at muzzle loading a single-shot shotgun. You will need a 209 primer adapter. Once you place this adapter in the breech of the gun, it is basically a long shotgun shell. You replace the primer in the adapter and then load the gun from the end of the barrel instead of loading a shell.

The additional thing you need is a ramrod to pack the barrel contents, and you can do away with any over wad/over shot cards and just use wool.

To load the gun, replace the spent primer in the adapter and close the breech. Load a measure of powder down the barrel. Then push a wad of wool down the barrel against the powder with the ramrod.

Next add a volume of shot followed by another wad and you are ready to shoot. Pretty simple really.

If you want to use a round ball you have molded, the first steps are the same: prime, powder, wad. Once this is done you will need a patch. This can be made from a square of bed sheet material just large enough to wrap around the ball. This creates a seal when pushed into the barrel and seated above the wad and shot.

TIPS AND TRICKS

- The versatility of this 12GA single-shot shotgun is truly amazing. As inexpensive as a used one is today, this makes it a vital piece of gear for any woodsman.
- A double-barrel break-open is a good option if you just think you must have a follow-up shot and the only main sacrifice there will be weight.
- My go-to company for subcaliber adapters is Short Lane Arms. Short Lane also makes a 209 shotgun primer adapter that makes your 12GA a muzzle loader if you choose. They also sell a retractable or breakdown ramrod that will fit in the haversack for use with the muzzle-loading system.
- For reloading shells, good quality high-brass shells will do better for this in the long run, or you can actually buy full brass 12 hulls online.
- Molds that will make a single round ball as well as ladles for melting lead shot over the fire can be purchased online from stores like Track of the Wolf.

— Chapter 13 —
TRAPPING: BEYOND THE BASICS

"In all things of nature there is something of the marvelous."
—ARISTOTLE

If you hope to catch some of your food, you should have a good working knowledge of traps for three main food sources: mammals, fish, and fowl.

One of the main concepts for longer-term living in the wild is that live food never spoils. For us it means that we are not forced to process the food straight away, only to care for it while we have it alive. This can be of big advantage in hot weather, but can also be troublesome if you're in an area with many large predatory animals. So a decision must be made. However for things like turtles and frogs, which can be kept in a sack or bag for a time, trapping is very advantageous.

Seasons and methods of take dictate what traps we can and cannot use as well as what species we can target. With traps being an indiscriminant means of catching prey we cannot control exactly what animal we catch; however, we can use traps sized, placed, and baited correctly for the target animal to reduce the risk of catching or killing a non-target animal. Check your local laws on what is to be done when a non-target animal is trapped.

BEGINNING WITH BAIT ANIMALS

The water's edge is the best place to secure meat sources the majority of the time. But first we have to realize that meat sources and trapping do not always have to involve four-legged furry critters. Some of the easiest meat we can obtain is from animals that live the majority of their lives in or near water, like fish, turtles, frogs, snakes, and crayfish.

Seeking these items of food for ourselves and then delegating a portion of them to bait the traps we build will enable us to catch more sizable prey items. If we are in an area absent of these water sources we will need to micro-trap to secure things like mice, rats, and chipmunks to effect the same end results. We could also choose to combine both techniques to our end benefit. Some of these resources will be meals in themselves as larger fish and turtles will fit this category as well.

Catching animals lower on the food chain should be a priority even if you don't plan to eat them yourself. A baited trap has a much higher percentage chance of success than a blind set. If you work your way up the food chain, you will fill your belly as you go and improve the food you eat along the way.

WATER-BASED TRAPS

You'll want to learn how to make and set traps in water so that you can catch animals like fish, frogs, and turtles.

NETS

Net-making is a skill all by itself that can take a lot of time to master. However, there are easy ways of creating nets (although these are not as effective as methods that require true net-making skills). Any net will only catch fish or animals that cannot exit the holes you have created, so many nets have to be tailored to the intended prey. In a pinch you can use a T-shirt as a seining device.

Here are some common types of nets that can be used in water:

- **Dip nets.** These nets are usually attached to some sort of hooped pole that can be used to reach into the water and lift the target out while trapped in the net. This pole can be fashioned from a green fork that is wrapped against itself to form the loop. The net is attached directly to this hoop while being made. If you are carrying a large roll of tarred mariners' bank line, which I highly recommend, you can easily fashion dip nets with overhand knots on a main line. You can use dip nets to catch small turtles but larger turtles are hard to approach with them. Remember that most turtles that flip into the water during the day will swim under the log they were sunning on to seek cover. Dip nets are also useful for frogging and for catching crayfish. See Figure 13.1.

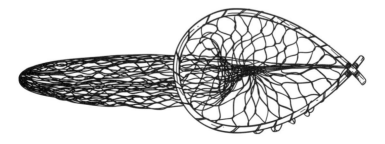

Figure 13.1 Dip net

- **Gill nets/stop nets.** This type net must be made long enough and deep enough to be stretched from one side of a creek or small river to the other and go from the top of the water to the bottom. It is usually weighted with stones at the bottom and has some type of floatation at the top or possibly a sapling running the length of the span. You drive fish into this net by walking downstream, chasing the fish into the net where they get hung in the holes as their gills pass through but body cannot. As with other nets, you will need to know the average size of the fish you're trapping to make an effective net. Dip nets and fishing traps tend to be a better use of cordage than a gill net/stop net. See Figure 13.2.

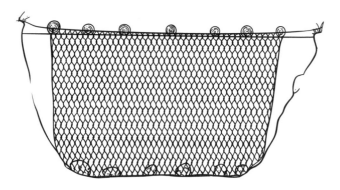

Figure 13.2 Gill net

- **Seine nets.** These are fairly large nets with very small holes that are walked through a deeper water source. They are used to manipulate smaller fish to the edge of the water to scoop them out. See Figure 13.3.

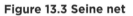

Figure 13.3 Seine net

Figure 13.4 Funnel net

- **Funnel nets.** These nets resemble dip nets in many ways and can be made in small diameter and elongated for fish-type traps or can be made in large diameter and laid flat to trap animals when the net is lifted. See Figure 13.4.

FISH FENCES

Fish fences can be used to either guide fish to a certain location in the water or placed on the water's edge for other types of animals like turtles. They can be built from any natural material including stones, sticks, or even logs. Fencing called a weir can be used to trap fish in a smaller area where you can hunt them with a bow or gig. An M-shaped bank trap allows a turtle to climb onto the bank for bait but will not allow it to return to the water. This is a good trap for overnight while you are asleep. See Figure 13.5.

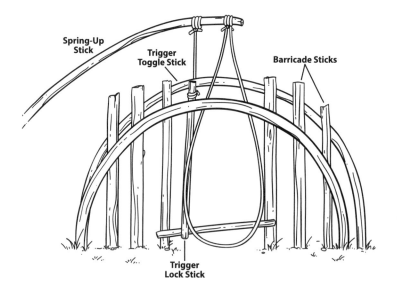

Figure 13.5 Fish fence

BASKET FUNNELS

Basket funnels are traps woven from natural materials employing two cones that fit together so that fish can swim in, yet they cannot swim out. These are woven in the same fashion as a basket. The inner cone has a hole in the bottom that fish can swim into, thus entering the closed larger cone, which traps them inside. See Figure 13.6.

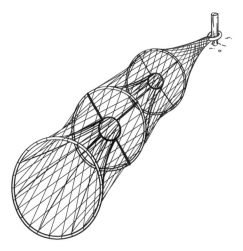

Figure 13.6 Basket funnel

TUBE TRAP

You can make a simple tube trap from any pop can by placing skewers into the can at an inward angle. These allow the animal in to eat the bait—but not back out again. See Figure 13.7.

Figure 13.7 Tube trap

SNARES

Fish can be caught with a snare-type device by using an available hook, bent safety pin, or carved gorge-type hook. Bait is easy enough to obtain; turn over logs until you find worms or grubs. You can also rig a trigger system so that the rod does not have to be attended. A simple hook with any red fabric chard will attract frogs to a hook and line.

LINES WITH L7 TRIGGERS

This is a form of fishing that employs line and trap together to set the hook after the animal runs with the bait. An L7 trigger (a type of quick-release system made with simple reverse notches, described in the section in trigger traps later in this chapter) is combined with a spring pole device, allowing the line to be hand cast off the bank with a baited hook of some sort. When the fish or turtle runs with the bait it dislodges the L7 trigger and springs the pole, which immediately jerks the line to set or lodge the hook in the throat of the prey. This trigger system can also be used to catch turtles. See Figure 13.8.

Figure 13.8 Trigger

Once you've secured one or more of the lower-food-chain meat sources (the things other mammals eat), you can use the leftover material for baiting traps to capture larger animals.

PRIMITIVE TRAPS

Primitive traps are designed to accomplish one or more of three things: strangle, mangle, or dangle. With that said, we need to look at the differing types of traps because many of the same releases or triggering systems can be employed with many different setups to accomplish the end goal.

DEADFALL TRAPS

These traps are often what you think of when you think of a primitive trap. They are generally designed to drop a large, heavy weight onto an animal, crushing it or trapping it beneath the weight of the deadfall. Small mammals such as mice, rats, chipmunks, and ground squirrels are about the largest animals that can easily be taken by deadfall traps. These animals are usually too small to set off more complicated spring-type traps (discussed in the following section).

Many people, unfortunately, set deadfalls incorrectly. There are many factors we must first realize about these traps to use them effectively. Deadfall traps are not always intended to instantly kill prey. Smaller deadfalls for micro-trapping of rodent species will many times suffocate the animal. Misunderstanding this point is what causes so many people to raise a deadfall like a rock or log at a high angle to achieve this crushing power. The fact is that the higher the angle of the deadfall, the more chance the animal has to escape the trap. Placing the bait as far to the back of the trap as possible will decrease the margin of error.

There are several different types of traps that use weight to kill or trap an animal:

- **Leaning deadfalls.** These traps generally employ a heavy object leaning at one end on the ground with the weight of the leaning object held up by a trigger that releases the weight of the deadfall. There are two simple rules of thumb when using these leaning deadfall devices. The first is that deadfalls should be five times heavier than the weight of the animal to be trapped, and the second is that the deadfall should never be at an angle greater than 30° from the ground. See Figure 13.9.

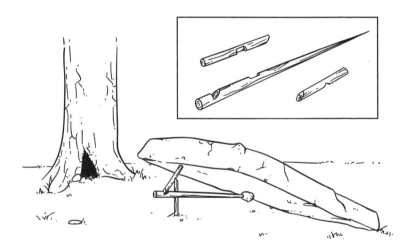

Figure 13.9 Leaning deadfall trap

- **Suspended deadfalls.** These traps involve a device suspended above the ground that drops upon release. These can also be combined with some type of spikes or spear points for larger game. See Figure 13.10.

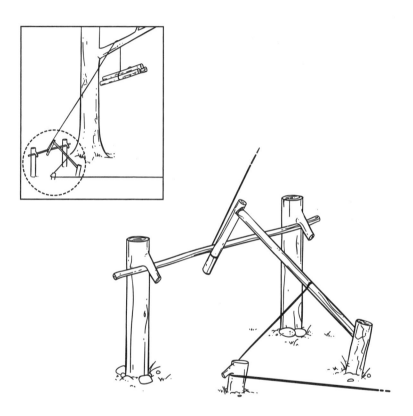

Figure 13.10 Suspended deadfall trap

- **Windlass machine traps.** These traps involve a windlass machine (a type of winch) that delivers a killing blow or deploys a spike or spear to impale the animal upon release of the trigger. See Figure 13.11.

Figure 13.11 Windlass machine trap

SNARES

A snare is a noose made of rope or wire that loops around an animal and pulls tight, catching it. Most snares will not catch the animal around the neck as you would hope. Body catches will happen more often than not. Snare loops need to be set at a targeted diameter to ensure a proper catch. A snare set a bit larger than an opossum's head will most likely never catch a coyote. This is another reason paying attention to animal sign is important. Only a baited and triggered snare should be set off trail (otherwise you are unlikely to catch anything), so this is an important consideration as well.

Medium-sized mammals like opossum and raccoon are about the largest animals you will want to tackle in a short-term situation since they can be processed and consumed easily without having a lot of meat lying around camp, something that will attract predatory or scavenging mammals. When trapping larger animals, set traps just off the trail going to or from a water source so that a non-target larger animal like a deer does not trip over and set off your trap unnecessarily. See Figure 13.12.

Figure 13.12 Snare

- **Free-hanging snares.** These are also call blind snares. They are unpowered snares that rely strictly on the animal's momentum or its fighting the trap to tighten and hold the creature. These are the least effective traps when done in primitive fashion; however, cable snares can be very effective. They can be set in small-game trails and should be suspended bearing in mind the animal's height at the head when walking. We always strive for a neck catch when snaring. For opossum or raccoon, if you can place your balled fist under the snare, that will be pretty close to head height. You want the opening of the snare for these animals to be about half again larger than your fist.
- **Powered snares.** Snares involving a spring-loaded engine or a counterweight device can be very effective depending on setup as long as they lift the animal off the ground. Remember, an animal will do what it has to for escape if it is alive and chewing is a natural act! If it is on the ground, it has lots of opportunity to chew its way free. (For this reason, trappers sometimes use wire or cable snares.)

Spring-loaded snares should always be alarmed for immediate reaction to reduce the suffering of the animal as well as to prevent its escape from the trap. All spring snares will require an engine or catalyst to make the snare close around the animal. Many things can be used for this, from a simple bent sapling to a counterweight device such as a log. Items from your kit can also make great engines, including bungee cords or sling-shot-type latex bands.

TRAP TRIGGERS

Trap triggers come in a variety of configurations. The main thing to remember is that triggers, like traps, must match the size of the quarry. Triggers for rodents cannot be made from 2" branches that the animal does not have the strength to pull down or manipulate to set off the trap. While there are many styles of these spring-type traps, I find the simpler the design and the simpler the trigger, the better. A pressure-release toggle can be adapted to several applications, and the majority of components can easily be carved in camp. In an extreme emergency, the toggle-type traps can be constructed with no tools at all. See Figures 13.13A, 13.13B, and 13.13C.

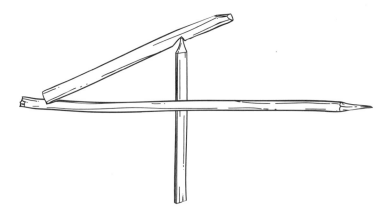

Figure 13.13A Figure 4 trigger

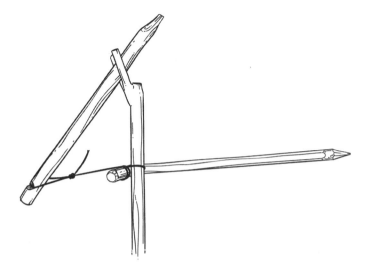

Figure 13.13B Piute trigger

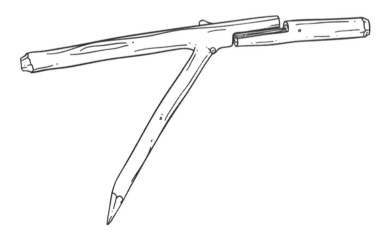

Figure 13.13C Split trigger

TRAPPING BIRDS

All North American birds are edible. Because of this—as well as the sheer number of them—birds can be a good choice to add to the table. Birds, especially small birds, should be trapped in an open clearing where the visibility of bait is optimal. Most of the time bright-colored berries or fruit will be most attractive to birds as bait. Remember to alarm the trap if possible, as the bird will be captured alive. There are three traps that work the best.

MULTIPLE GROUND SNARES

One of the most effective traps for small-seed-feeding birds is a simple stake in the ground surrounded by a small pile of ground debris with small-diameter snares attached that overlap to create a network of ground snares. Bait them with something the birds are feeding on. Two main considerations here are:

1. The size of snare material should be very fine line.
2. You need many snares—at least 25 for a 2-square-foot area with 2–3" overlapping loops. See Figure 13.14.

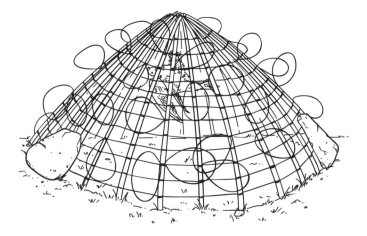

Figure 13.14 Multiple ground snares

OJIBWA BIRD TRAP

This trap uses a perch for the bird to land. The weight of the bird on the perch drops a counterweight that, when released, activates the snare, which in turn traps the bird by its feet. This device works well as the bird will grab the stick when landing, ensuring its legs are inside the snare (which lies over the perching stick). The big trick to this snare is to make sure that the closed snare is drawn close to the hole in the upright pole so that the bird is held tight and close in an upside-down position. See Figure 13.15.

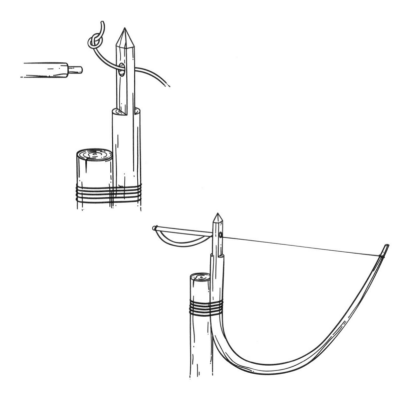

Figure 13.15 Ojibwa bird trap

CAGE-STYLE TRAPS

Cage-style traps for smaller birds are easily built by making an X with a length of cord across two sticks, then filling in with progressively shorter lengths of cord in log-cabin fashion. Small tripping lines work well connected to a step or breakaway trigger so that birds attempt to hop or duck the strings to get to seed bait in the center of the trap. This trap can catch up to ten birds in an hour in the right conditions. See Figure 13.16.

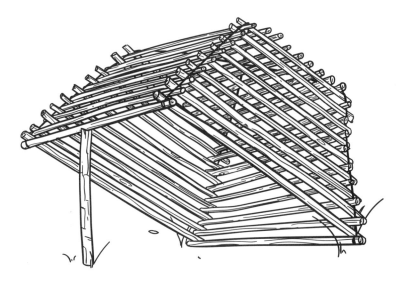

Figure 13.16 Cage trap

You can also take a larger bird with a net, especially at night. During nesting season, most waterbirds like geese or ducks will defend their nest to the point of becoming very vulnerable to dispatch. This gives you the opportunity for eggs as well.

EATING ANIMALS FOUND DEAD

Okay, so what about animals we find already dead? A free meal, right? Maybe. There are several things you must consider before digging in. First, realize that heat is the enemy of any fresh meat even if the animal was healthy when it died, so the longer it has been dead the more you should think before eating. However, you can put a lot of trust in your own nose. We can tell when something smells off. When it does, stay clear of it.

With fish the best indicator is the gills. If they are still pink, the meat should be okay. Once they turn white, don't consume it, even if it's well cooked.

What about mammals? I have a personal policy that unless it is an extreme emergency I will not eat any mammal I did not see expire. This allows me to evaluate the way it died or was killed as well as the condition that animal may have been in before expiring. It may have died from a disease. Some diseases are transmittable to humans, and you want to avoid them. If the animal is not acting according to normal behavior, there is usually a reason for it. For example, raccoons are nocturnal animals. To see one wandering around during the heat of the day is an automatic red flag to me.

If you must eat an animal you find dead, there are some things to take note of to determine how long it has been dead as well. However, there are no guarantees.

- If the animal is bloated badly, it has likely been there a while and is no good.
- If there are still fleas on the carcass, it has not been dead long as these will be the first to abandon a dead host.
- If the eyes are still wet or glossy, this is a good indicator of an animal that has died recently.
- If there are maggots on the body, this is a sign it has been dead too long.

- If you decide to clean and eat the animal, look at the internal organs for bright rich coloring. If the liver has any spots on it or there are lumps visible on the organs, abandon that desire to eat and move on.

One thing to remember about a road-killed animal is there's a good chance the internal organs were damaged, including the bladder, which may taint any interior meats as well.

RECIPES FOR TRAPPED GAME

The following are some of my favorite recipes to use for trapped game.

FRIED POTATOES AND SQUIRREL

Boiling the squirrel the night before reduces the amount of time it takes to make this meal.

1 squirrel, skinned and gutted
½ teaspoon Old Bay Seasoning or garlic powder
2 medium russet potatoes
1 onion
Bacon grease or lard for pan frying

Boil squirrel in pot the night before. The meat is ready when it is falling from the bone. Drain and debone. Store the meat in a cool place, away from scavengers or predators.

The next day, shred the squirrel meat and mix with Old Bay Seasoning.

Boil potatoes for approximately 15 minutes, then slice. Dice the onion.

Grease a pan with bacon grease or lard and heat over medium heat. Add onion, potatoes, and squirrel meat to the pan and fry until the meat is heated through and the potatoes are golden brown. Serve.

DUTCH OVEN RACCOON ROAST

*This is a great meal to start in the morning
and then enjoy for an evening meal.*

3–4 pounds fresh raccoon meat, cut into chunks
4–6 tablespoons cooking oil
1 beef bouillon cube or 2 teaspoons beef bouillon powder
1 cup hot water
3 medium potatoes, quartered
3 medium carrots, peeled and cut into 1½" pieces
2 medium onions, quartered
Old Bay Seasoning or other seasoning to taste

In a Dutch oven over hot coals, braise raccoon meat in oil. Dissolve bouillon in hot water to make broth.

Once the raccoon meat is browned, add vegetables, broth, and seasonings.

Cover and cook over medium heat 3–5 hours or until meat reaches desired level of doneness.

RABBIT STEW

This is a good stew recipe that can work with most types of game.

1 large rabbit or 2 young ones, butchered into 8 pieces
6 pieces salt-cured bacon, cut up
4 large carrots, peeled and cut into chunks
8 red potatoes, quartered
2 cloves garlic, minced
½ cup apple cider vinegar
1 medium onion, diced
2 tablespoons butter
3 tablespoons all-purpose flour
2 teaspoons salt
2 teaspoons ground black pepper

Place rabbit in stew pot and cover with water. Bring to a boil and boil for about 5 minutes. Add all ingredients along with enough water to cover the meat in the pot. Slow cook over medium heat 1 hour. Serve with bread or biscuits.

OPOSSUM ROAST

*As with any roast, baste this one frequently
with drippings to retain moistness.*

1 small opossum, cleaned and quartered
1 teaspoon salt
2 tablespoons lemon juice
1 teaspoon ground black pepper
1 teaspoon Old Bay Seasoning
Dash Cholula Hot Sauce
1 tablespoon Worcestershire sauce

Place opossum in a Dutch oven. Mix remaining ingredients into a paste and spread over the opossum.

Roast using medium heat 30 minutes per pound, usually about 2–3 hours. Baste frequently with drippings. Serve with drop biscuits.

OPOSSUM CRACKLINGS

*This works best with a winter opossum, as it will have more fat. Be careful
not to overheat or burn as this will impart a bad flavor.*

1 opossum

Remove fat from the opossum. Use the meat in another recipe.

Place fat in a skillet and render by cooking on medium heat.

Pour off the liquid and save for lard. The hard brown bits leftover are cracklings. They eat well when salted or seasoned with Old Bay.

GLAZED PHEASANT

This recipe can work for a larger bird.

2 pheasants
¼ cup salt
1 box wild rice stuffing mixture (12 ounces), prepared according to package directions
1 jar raspberry preserves (about 12 ounces)
½ cup water

Remove feathers from birds. Rinse birds, remove giblets, and pat dry. Sprinkle cavity with salt, and stuff with dressing. Tie legs together with string and arrange in a Dutch oven. Bake 1½–2 hours or until tender.

Mix preserves and water in a pan and bring to boil. During the last ½ hour of baking, baste the birds frequently with the preserve mixture. Remove strings before serving with remaining preserves.

TIPS AND TRICKS

- Frogs are fairly easy to stun with any flexible stick if hunted at night with a headlight to freeze them in place. This technique will work whether the frog is on land or in water.
- Snakes will be found in the water or on the edge, especially at night when frogs are present. They can be dispatched just like a frog with a nice flexible stick. Or, you can pin them down with a Y-shaped branch and dispatch them with a rock. However, trapping a snake is tough, as they are masters of escape.
- Alarming of any trap possible is important.
- The location of traps is also important. Try to keep all traps within a 50–100-yard perimeter of your camp so you can easily get to them in the middle of the night if you catch

something. Scavenger animals such as opossums and raccoons are not shy of humans for long, and scent control is not a worry with them.

- Travel routes are excellent places for traps. Prey can often be lured to a baited trap as most are opportunistic in nature.
- You may at some time capture a non-target animal. If it is a large animal, it will most likely escape without your help. If it is a skunk, you are one step away from a few days of good stink, but so goes life in an emergency scenario. Just do your best to free the animal and watch its back end!

— Chapter 14 —
BUTCHERING GAME

"Cook ingredients that you are used to cooking by other techniques, such as fish, chicken, or hamburgers. In other words be comfortable with the ingredients you are using."

—BOBBY FLAY

Understanding the basic principles behind cleaning and butchering is an important aspect of cooking. This process can have a positive or negative effect on not only taste but also the freshness of the meat you intend to cook.

It is fair enough to say that any animal killed should have the guts removed at the soonest opportunity as heat is a bacteria-growing paradise. Once an animal is dead, the quality of the meat decreases exponentially without proper care.

CONDITIONS OF THE KILL

To start, we should think about temperature when we harvest game. Refrigerators are designed to preserve food, and they are set at around 38–40°F in most cases. So, logically if we harvest meat in a temperature warmer than this we need some urgency in the processing to keep the food in good condition.

There are many mitigating factors to the condition even of freshly killed meat. These include the animal's health, time of year, age and sex of animal, as well as the timeliness of its death. If an animal runs hard or is scared just prior to dying and its adrenaline is flowing, the meat will not be as good as meat of an animal killed instantly in a calm state. These are all things to consider when taking game.

An animal killed quickly (whether by trapping or hunting) should provide very good-quality meat if it is recovered in good time.

Fish don't present the same worries. Fighting a fish to land it does not affect its quality. Just process it quickly after the catch.

BUTCHERING TOOLS

Tools of the butcher are as diverse as for a professional of any kind. However, you need not worry too much about this for camp meat as you will not be doing the detail of the processing butchers do to sell select cuts of meat. You will need certain tools, but most of these you will have already in your kit if you are camping anyway.

KNIFE

A good sharp knife of a butchering style with a 5" blade will handle up to the largest game. A fillet knife is handy if fish will be on the menu. A pocketknife with a smaller blade will help in the process but is not a necessity for down-and-dirty processing of meat for the fire. Ulu-type blades, which are crescent shaped, are used in many countries and are a handy camp kitchen tool, though not crucial to the process. A large cleaver is convenient if you have a mind to carry one but a good hatchet will work as well.

AXE

A camp hatchet or axe will suffice for lots of quickly needed tasks like foot and head removal and can also aid in further bone cutting and skinning if needed. Keep your axe as sharp as your knife. A hunter's-style axe has a rounded pole on the back to aid in pushing between the hide and the carcass on larger animals.

BUSHCRAFT TIP

If you are carrying a large blade such as a machete-type tool, this can easily replace the axe for most chores that require one.

SHEARS

Again this may be something already in your kit, but a good set of heavy sewing shears can come in right handy at times when processing fowl. Shears make quick work of opening a body cavity on small game and are also of good use on fowl with hollow bones that are easily clipped to separate the pieces, like wings from the carcass or discards like feet.

SAW

A good saw is an asset to any camp, but the blade choice and type of saw is important for this task. A good bone-cutting blade is expensive, but if you carry a cheap 12" bucking saw with a metal tubular frame, you can buy equally inexpensive hacksaw blades that make great bone-cutting blades. So this can be another item in camp that works for more than one chore.

GAMBREL/MEAT HOOK

Some type of gambrel or at least a meat hook will be needed to raise the animal high enough off the ground to make the job of butchering easy and to keep the carcass out of the dirt. For larger animals, you may need a come-along or winch. Simple block-and-tackle systems are easy enough to craft in a pinch with minimal equipment. You need a rope, something to act as the axle (such as a sturdy tree branch—still attached to the tree), and something to tie the rope to once the load has been lifted.

SAFETY CONCERNS

Any time you're handling an animal carcass it's a good idea to wear some sort of disposable gloves to protect against bacteria entering cuts and scratches on your hands while working with raw meat.

- **Meat freshness.** As far as the freshness of meat, you should trust your nose a lot. If you have questions, give it a smell. If in doubt, don't eat it.
- **Aging meat.** Aging the meat—the process of holding meat at a temperature of 34–40°F for 7–10 days—breaks down proteins and can make game meats a bit more palatable and tender. However, it is not a very easy or exact science in camp. Better to just cook it and deal with possible toughness by the way it is prepared. If you are in the woods to eat wild meat, fresh is the best and safest eating for my money.

PROCESSING CONSIDERATIONS

For larger game animals that may hang for a day or two in camp while being processed slowly for camp meals, the skin should be left on the carcass after gutting and only removed when being processed. This will keep the meat from drying out and help keep any possible bugs off the surface. However, this is only a good practice in cooler temps—remember the refrigerator conversation. Small game can be processed and cooked immediately as the cooked meat will be less likely to spoil after cooking.

Meat can also be kept cool by placing the processed cuts into a plastic watertight bag, removing as much air as possible and storing it in the creek (depending on water temperature), held down by rocks or logs, and tied to a limb or root so it doesn't wash away.

BUSHCRAFT TIP

For any mammal, the true key is keeping the meat from being contaminated after the kill. Urine, feces, or other liquids contained within the lower digestive organs should never come in contact with the meat or it can change the taste dramatically.

THE BUTCHERING PROCESS

In larger animals like deer, as soon as the animal is dead, you should put on your gloves, place the animal on its side, take your knife and cut deep around the anus, and on a doe the vulva, then pull this material out and tie it off with a cord or zip tie to prevent contamination.

While gutting take great care not to perforate the lower organs with your knife.

Once this is done roll the deer onto its back with the rear end facing downhill if possible and insert your knife into the body of the deer just below the breastbone, at an angle toward the neck so that you don't puncture the stomach, and open an air gap in the body cavity.

Once this hole is created, withdraw the knife and insert your fingers in a V to guide the knife in cutting shallowly in the other direction all the way to the pelvis.

You can remove the external male organs at this point. You can also remove the internal organs, cutting away any connective tissue from the body cavity, and any leftover material in the pelvis area. Then hang the deer for further processing.

SMALL MAMMALS

With any other mammal, the process is much the same with less mess and work as they get smaller. Remove head and feet, then gut the animal. Small game such as rabbit and squirrel can be skinned without hanging easy enough by making a cut through the fur across the backbone and pulling by hand in opposite directions.

SMALL GAME BIRDS

Small game birds are easy enough to breast by standing the bird on the wings, keeping your feet close to the body of the bird, then bending over and pulling up on the feet. This will separate the carcass and expose the breast meat.

LARGER GAME BIRDS

Larger birds like turkey and duck are treated a bit differently. Gut them by cutting just below the breastbone and slicing all the way down to the anus, then removing the innards. As with mammals, be careful not to cut into the intestines. If you want to remove the feathers before eating, do so soon after harvesting and before beginning the butchering.

TIPS AND TRICKS

- I use some type of food-grade oil on my tools all the time in case I am going to process food with them. The oil protects the tools from rust; using food-grade oil means I won't ingest anything toxic. In salt-water environments stainless steel is best but I find carbon much easier to maintain in the field.

- The task of skinning and processing meat requires sharp tools, so an assortment of sharpening aids, like a diamond rod, steel, and carborundum for the axe, will be very useful.
- When breaking down an animal, use the anatomical lines already in place to guide your knife. Cut along muscle groups (instead of through them) and between bones instead of trying to hack your way through.
- Remember that any items left from the butchering that you are not using can become bait for other meals and traps, as well as an attractant for hunting later.
- Be careful to avoid cross-contamination when butchering raw meat. When possible, use dedicated tools for the job, and clean your tools carefully before using them for other processes.

Chapter 15

CATCHING FISH AND FROGS

"Fishing is much more than fish. It is the great occasion when we may return to the fine simplicity of our forefathers."

—HERBERT HOOVER

Fish, frogs, and crayfish are probably the easiest meat sources of high quality to secure in the wild from most areas. Rod and reel are often carried by campers. I would also suggest a frog gig if you plan to secure camp meat even when the fish may not be biting.

FISHING EQUIPMENT

Equipment for fishing can be as simple as a hand line or as complicated as the most expensive and modern rod/ reel combo. However, there are some real nice packages for packable rods and reels that can be found fairly inexpensively. A light-action rod will work for most around-the-camp fishing from shore and something of less than 6' will do fine.

Tests of line should probably range from 4–6 pounds so that they are durable yet strong in case you are fishing for bluegill and happen to hook a lurking bass in the shallows.

BUSHCRAFT TIP

To make a bottle trap to catch bait, cut off the shoulders and neck of a plastic bottle (any size) and invert it so that the cut ends come together, creating a funnel. You can sew the pieces together with fishing line or tape the edges together with duct tape if you're worried they'll come apart. Weight the bottle with a few stones, add some bait (such as insects), and place it in shallow water. Secure it into position with more fishing line. Once fish swim in, they won't be able to swim out again and you can use them as bait for larger, more desirable fish.

For tackle, keep it simple. Live bait can often be found near shore and captured with a dip net or bottle trap, so hooks and weights (sinkers) are about all you need with a couple of floats or strike indicators.

In all the fishing I have done around the eastern woodland areas the most productive artificial bait I have found is a simple inline spinner such as a Mepps or Rooster Tail. They are attractive to almost all species of pan and game fish and they are an easy lure to use. Just cast and reel, varying the speed and the depth till you find the fish.

Choose a few standard colors, like yellow, white, and chartreuse green, in about ⅛ ounce, plus something that looks very natural as well like a brown or dark red. This should serve you well.

FROG AND FISH KIT

A simple kit made from any cylindrical object, be it a soda can or PVC tube, will increase your odds greatly and add a new dimension to your fun in the outdoors. This kit is created using an 8" piece of ¾" PVC with an end plug glued into one side and a removable cap at the other. All components can be stored inside the tube when not in use.

In the cap, drill a hole large enough to secure a wrist loop of paracord. On the outside, I recommend about 50 yards of 50-pound spider wire. This fishing line is small enough in diameter to secure small fish but also heavy enough for the occasional big boy you may hook.

I recommend the following: 5 #6 hooks and 5 #8 hooks, several split shot, and a couple of small bobbers. I also carry about 12" of red yarn; frogs can't resist this wrapped around a hook and dangled in front of them. Remember that big hooks catch big fish but small hooks catch a lot of fish!

With this kit, you gain a lot of confidence very quickly.

BREADED FROG SKEWERS

This is one of my favorite ways to fix frog—and it's quick and easy.

4–5 frogs, fresh caught
1 box hush puppy mix (about 10 ounces), prepared according to package directions
Hot sauce, to taste

Cut frogs at the hind quarters and roll in hush puppy mix. Skewer with a green stick and cook over medium coals till golden brown, about 10 minutes.

Shake a bit of Louisiana or Cholula Hot sauce on the frog legs as you eat, discarding the bones.

PREPARING FROGS AND FISH

Frogs are fairly simple to prepare. We will only consume the back legs in most cases and these can easily be cut free at the uppermost joint from the carcass. Once the legs are removed, the skin is easily peeled off and the legs are ready for cooking.

Filleting or prepping fish can be done in several ways. The simplest is to cut the fish from vent through the gills and remove everything inside to include the gills. The fish can then be cooked or further prepared by either beheading or filleting or both.

To fillet the fish is to remove the most usable meat and discard the rest. Make a cut the width of the fish just on the outside of the gill plate on both sides of the fish. Then take the tip of a sharp knife and working on either side of the backbone begin to cut along the top of the ribs. Once this meat is freed it will still be connected at the tail and you can flip the entire slab over and use a long flexible blade to cut between the meat and the skin so that you are left with only a slab of fresh fish with no bones or skin. This is called the fillet. See Figure 15.1.

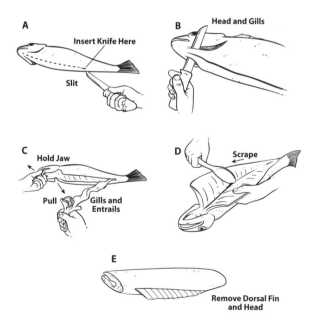

Figure 15.1 How to clean fish

Lots of fish are easily cooked whole after removing the gills and cuts, and the meat can then be picked from the carcass with a fork to avoid the bones. Fish cooked in foil over coals will separate very well from the skin, and this locks in all of the flavor as well.

TIPS AND TRICKS

- The thing with many fishing lures is they seem to catch a lot more people than they do fish. Limit yourself to just a few types that will cover multiple water depths and retrieve speeds, and have confidence you will catch fish. To me, confidence is more important than any lure you use.
- Use your ears. You can often hear frogs before you see them.
- Keep frogs and fish alive so you don't have to immediately process them. A 5-gallon bucket with a lid, filled with water, will hold them until you can get to them. Cut air holes in the lid.
- Patience and persistence are key in both frogging and fishing. If you're not successful on a first pass, you might be successful on a second.
- Make sure before setting out that you check local laws and regulations as well as acquire any necessary licenses or permissions.

Chapter 16

DAVE'S FAVORITE RECIPES

"Fat gives things flavor."

—Julia Child

OLD RELIABLES

These recipes have stood the test of time.

SAUSAGE NUGGETS

Serve with pan-fried hash browns for a hearty meal.

1 pound ground sausage, any type
1 pound sharp Cheddar cheese, grated
3 cups Bisquick
½ teaspoon Old Bay Seasoning

Mix together all ingredients and roll into small balls, about black walnut size. Cook in a greased Dutch oven 10–15 minutes or until done (no pink in center).

SURVIVAL BREAD

This no-frills bread will fill you up if you run low on other food supplies.

3 cups all-purpose flour
1 teaspoon salt
1 package (¼ ounce) active dry yeast
2¼ cups water
Small amount of fat, such as lard or vegetable oil

Mix together the dry ingredients. Warm the water to about 110°F (too hot or too cold and the yeast won't activate). If you don't have a thermometer, water of this temperature is about what you'd want for a nice warm shower—not too hot, not too cold.

Slowly add water to dry ingredients while mixing to form a dough consistency. Cover with a rag and let stand in a warm place for 24 hours (90–100°F). Dough should double in size.

Working on a floured board, knead about 6–8 times. Grease the dough with lard or vegetable oil and shape into a loaf. Cut a cross in the top of the loaf and let stand for about 1 hour.

If cooking in a Dutch oven, use fewer bottom coals and double on the top of the lid. Rotate the lid about every 5 minutes and cook 20 minutes on medium heat. You can also cook in a loaf pan or other type of cooking pot, but use a lid, or form a lid from aluminum foil, to help trap the heat and cook the bread thoroughly. It's done when it makes a hollow sound when tapped on the top.

CAT HEAD BISCUITS

For kids, a fun variation on this recipe is to form the dough around the end of a stick and cook it over the campfire, then pull it off and eat.

3 cups all-purpose flour
4 teaspoons baking powder
1 teaspoon salt
¼ teaspoon baking soda
1 cup lard (or butter or shortening)
1 cup buttermilk

Mix dry ingredients together. Cut in lard and add buttermilk.

Mix to a formable dough and knead 8 times on a floured board. Roll out or flatten by hand so dough is about 1" thick.

Cut out biscuits by hand or use an opened can to cut them out. Biscuits should be about 3–4" in diameter.

Cook in a greased Dutch oven about 20 minutes.

To make buttermilk, add 1 tablespoon lemon juice or vinegar to 1 cup milk and stir.

MOUNTAIN MAN BREAKFAST

For those mornings when you've got a big appetite!

4 large russet potatoes (any kind will do), cut into chunks
½ tube of sausage such as Jimmy Dean Premium Pork Sausage or 8 ounces sausage, sliced or crumbled
6 eggs
½ pound medium Cheddar cheese, grated

In a Dutch oven, boil potatoes until partially cooked, about 10–15 minutes.

While potatoes are boiling, cook sausage in a skillet until cooked through, about 8–10 minutes. Remove sausage from skillet; set aside.

Add eggs to sausage fat in skillet and scramble.

Drain potatoes. Add eggs and sausage to potatoes in Dutch oven. Add cheese. Cover and cook 20 minutes on medium heat.

SCOTCH EGGS

This hearty meal doesn't have to be for breakfast!

4 large hard-boiled eggs, shells removed
1 pound ground sausage, any kind
1¼ cups corn flour, wheat flour, or bread crumbs
Salt, ground black pepper, and other seasonings of choice to taste
2 fresh eggs
2–3 cups oil (your choice) for frying

Dry hard-boiled eggs with a towel or rag. Pat sausage into thin patties and wrap each egg completely.

Mix together flour and seasonings in a shallow dish.

Break the fresh eggs into another shallow dish and scramble well.

Dip sausage-egg roll in egg and then roll in breading mix.

Fry in oil in a Dutch oven until golden brown, about 5 minutes, turning halfway through. Serve.

9-BEAN SOUP

If using dried beans without seasoning, add 2–3 teaspoons Old Bay Seasoning.

1 bag mixed soup beans with seasoning (about 20 ounces)
1 pound salt-cured bacon, diced

Add beans to Dutch oven and cover with water. Bring to a boil over medium or medium-high coals. Boil 10 minutes.

Add bacon. Boil an additional 10 minutes, then move to low-heat part of fire and cook 1 hour.

HOBO STEW

This favorite uses up all your leftovers. I make this in a bush pot for myself.

Leftover meat
1–2 large potatoes
2–3 tablespoons dried vegetables or leftover vegetables
Old Bay Seasoning or your preference, to taste

In a Dutch oven or bush pot, cook whatever meat is left over in camp by boiling until tender.

Add more liquid after boiling to raise pot back to ¾ full. Add potatoes and vegetables.

Cook until all contents are heated through and water is reduced to about ¼ of the pot, about 30 minutes. You can add instant potatoes for a thickener if the stew is thin. Season to taste and serve.

CAMP JAMBALAYA

You can use any seafood for this jambalaya.

1 package ground sausage (about 16 ounces)
8–12 fresh crawfish (tail meat only)
1 bag precooked rice (8–9 ounces), (I like Uncle Ben's Butter & Garlic Ready Rice)
2 medium onions, diced
3 green bell peppers, seeded and diced
2 tablespoons Old Bay Seasoning
¼ teaspoon cayenne pepper
½ cup water

Brown sausage in a Dutch oven. Add remaining ingredients and simmer 30 minutes or until rice is cooked through. Serve.

BREAD PUDDING

This Bread Pudding goes great with Camp Jambalaya.

8 slices stale bread
2 eggs or powdered equivalent
¼ teaspoon salt
2 cups milk
¼ cup butter
½ cup granulated sugar
2 teaspoons ground cinnamon or nutmeg
½ cup fresh raspberries
Topping of your choice—cinnamon, brown sugar, or molasses

Cut bread into small cubes and set aside. In a small bowl, beat eggs and salt together and set aside.

Place milk and butter in a 2-quart saucepan and heat until scalded.

In a large bowl, add bread, sugar, cinnamon, and egg mixture. Slowly add milk and butter mixture. Stir until bread is well soaked. Stir in raspberries.

Pour mixture into a small Dutch oven or pot and bake 30–45 minutes or until golden brown on top and heated all the way through. Top with cinnamon, brown sugar, or molasses and serve.

RASPBERRY COBBLER

S'mores aren't the only way to satisfy your sweet tooth at a campfire!

¼ cup butter, melted
¾ cup all-purpose flour
¾ cup granulated sugar
¾ cup milk
2 cups fresh raspberries (any fruit will work for this; if using canned fruit, strain first)

Mix all ingredients except fruit into a batter. Pour batter into a Dutch oven. Scatter in the fruit. Cook 1 hour over medium heat or until bubbling.

QUICK FAVORITES

These recipes cook up fast—but they're still full of flavor.

PIGS IN A BLANKET

Use a stick to cook these just like marshmallows over the fire.

8–10 link sausages or 3–4 hot dogs or 1 kielbasa sausage, cut into 4 pieces
1 package quick 3-cheese biscuit mix (about 7½ ounces), prepared according to package directions

Boil sausage or hot dogs in water 6–10 minutes, until cooked through. Remove from water and pat dry.

Roll the prepared dough into a rectangle and cut into strips about 1" wide. Wrap the dough around the sausages like a ribbon spiraling the sausage.

Place on a stick and cook over medium coals for 5 minutes, turning constantly. Eat right off the stick or dip in a ranch dressing.

SAUSAGE KABOBS

For a different flavor, try adding pineapple chunks to the kabob.

3–4 smoked sausage links, cut into 2" slices
4 new red potatoes, quartered
1 green bell pepper, seeded and sliced

Thread sausage, potatoes, and peppers onto skewers or a stick, alternating ingredients. Cook over medium coals until sausage and potatoes are cooked well.

TINFOIL TROUT

This dish can work for any fish. Substitute ramps for the onion if you prefer.

1 fresh-caught trout
1 medium onion, sliced
3 tablespoons butter, sliced
Garlic, salt, and ground black pepper to taste

After gutting the trout, lay on heavy foil with enough on all sides to completely fold over the fish. Place onions, butter, garlic, salt, and pepper in cavity. Fold foil over and crimp shut so juices don't escape.

Cook on top of coal bed about 10 minutes, turning once. When done skin should peel off easy and meat should fall off the bone.

MARCI'S BEST

A very good friend of mine, Marci Waleff, is a Viking re-enactor (she goes by the name Mistress Marsi of Hadley) and a great outdoor cook. She generously shared some of her best outdoor cooking recipes with us.

FARMER CHEESE

This simple cheese recipe is a fun camp activity.
Reserve the whey produced in this recipe for other uses.

1 gallon whole milk (not ultrapasteurized)
½ cup vinegar
Sea salt or smoked salt to taste

Set up your workstation with a cheesecloth or linen cloth in your whey-catching bucket.

Heat milk over the fire to the boiling point. Remove from fire as soon as it boils.

Quickly add vinegar and stir. You will see the milk curdle and the solids separate from the liquid.

At the workstation, lift the curds into the cheese cloth. I use a simple linen cloth or large cotton flour sack material. Once you have lifted the curds that will come out in a solid form, pour the remainder of the material slowly into your cloth-lined bucket. You may squeeze unwanted whey from the cloth or leave it to hang for an hour or so.

Add sea salt to taste and enjoy.

MARSI'S OATCAKE

This should keep for several weeks just wrapped in linen cloth provided you have used quality dried ingredients. If you use fresh fruit in lieu of dried fruit, your mix will be more moist; therefore, you should eat the oatcake within a week or so. As this ages it dries out, so it is a great traveler's companion.

¼ cup honey
½ cup lard or butter
4 cups of your favorite dried mix of all-natural oats, dried berries, fruit, grains, and nuts (you can even use all-natural organic granola)
2 pinches sea salt
½ –1 cup oat flour (do not use wheat flour)
Your favorite sweet spices such as cinnamon, ginger, nutmeg, cloves, pie spice, mace, etc. (I usually add at least 1 teaspoon or so of these spices combined. Spice as you see fit. You can experiment here.)
2 large eggs (optional)
½ cup brown sugar or cane sugar (optional)
½ cup dried/smoked meat, fresh fruit or berries, seeds, or cinnamon and sugar as topping (optional)

Place all ingredients in a bowl and pulverize. A potato masher, meat mallet, or heavy-duty wooden spoon works great. The consistency should mimic Play-Doh with rice. You can always add extra dry ingredients if too thin.

Grease 2 round cake pans or prewarmed Dutch ovens.

Divide mixture and press into cake pans or Dutch ovens. If desired you may top with seeds or cinnamon and sugar. Be sure to press any toppings into the cake.

Bake at medium to medium-low heat for about 30 minutes or until edges of oatcake begin to darken slightly and move away from the sides of the pan. If cooking in a Dutch oven, pull coals away from your main fire, sit Dutch oven on coals, pack coals around the edges, and lay coals on top.

Immediately after they are removed from the oven or fire you will need to press the cakes under a heavy weight. You can choose a flat rock or griddle and top with the Dutch ovens. Leave sit away from critters for several hours to overnight.

Enjoy! The older the oatcake gets the drier it becomes. However, lard will maintain its moisture longer than most fats. This is helpful in flavoring, consistency, and preservation.

HUSH PUPPIES

A delicious side when served with fish.

1 cup whole-wheat flour
1 cup cornmeal
1 cup whey, water, or milk
1 teaspoon baking soda
1 teaspoon sea salt (try smoked salt for even better flavor)
Hot oil or lard for frying

Mix all ingredients except oil together to the consistency of a thick cake batter.

Place lard or oil in cauldron or Dutch oven sitting on hot coals or hanging over the fire with consistent heat.

When oil is hot (a small piece of batter dropped into the oil sizzles) drop batter into oil by large spoonfuls.

Turn hush puppies several times to brown evenly, about 2–3 minutes each.

Remove and enjoy! Try various dips and toppings. I like vinegar on my hush puppies.

HORSERADISH SAUCE

Be careful in tasting and grating horseradish as it contains caustic oils that can burn the skin and eyes. Sauce is excellent when used to coat meat that you will flash-fry prior to roasting.

2 parts wild horseradish
1 part olive oil
Salt, to taste

Scrape the horseradish root with the back of your knife or grate. Macerate the horseradish greens. Add olive oil. Salt to taste and serve.

CURED FISH

Any fatty fish such as salmon or trout can be used.
I have personally used trout and salmon.

1 fresh-caught trout
1 cup salt
1 cup sugar
1 teaspoon ground white pepper
1 cup fresh dill or fresh mint

Clean your fish, leaving skin on.

Split fish down the center. Be sure to remove pin bones by running your hand down along the fish against the grain.

Mix together dry ingredients (not including the mint or dill). Rub dry ingredients onto flesh of fish. Sandwich dill or mint inside of fish.

Tie fish together with skin side out. Wrap in waxed linen, waxed paper, or plastic wrap.

Keep cool 3–5 days. Weather permitting, bury the whole operation 12–18" in the earth, or add this to your cooler or refrigerator with a weight on top.

After 3–5 days, remove, rinse, slice thin, and serve. For a hint of citrus in the out of doors, add wood sorrel leaves to your fish prior to serving.

BERRY CRISP

You can use any berries you like for this recipe—try a mix of several.

2–3 cups fresh or frozen berries
1 cup rolled or steel-cut oats
½ cup whole-wheat flour
½ cup brown sugar or organic cane sugar
½ cup butter, softened
1 teaspoon ground cinnamon

Put berries in the bottom of a well-seasoned Dutch oven. (If berries are very tart, top with a little sugar and cinnamon now.)

Mix together oats, flour, sugar, butter, and cinnamon. Top berries with this mixture.

Place in coals about 30 minutes or until berries are bubbling. Serve and enjoy!

EASY PEACH COBBLER

This recipe really couldn't be any easier!

1 can peaches (about 16 ounces)
1 package spice cake mix (about 15½ ounces)
½ cup butter, if desired

Empty can of peaches into Dutch oven, juice and all. Shake dry cake mix on top of peaches. If desired, place dabs of butter on top of cake mix.

Bury the Dutch oven in the coals for approximately 30–40 minutes until peaches are thick and bubbly.

EASY CHOCOLATE CHERRY LAVA COBBLER

Nothing goes better with the great outdoors than a little chocolate!

10 ounces Dr. Pepper or Coke
1 package chocolate cake mix (about 15½ ounces)
2 cans cherry pie filling (about 20 ounces each)

Preheat seasoned Dutch oven to medium.

Take a drink from a 12-ounce can of soda. Add soda to cake mix and mix slightly.

Empty pie filling into the bottom of Dutch oven. Spoon batter on top of cherries. Cover with lid.

Cover Dutch oven in coals and bake approximately 30–40 minutes or until cake is set.

TIPS AND TRICKS

- Cooking over a campfire or using a camp stove is not as predictable as using a regular stove or oven. Keep an eye on your meal, and don't be afraid to turn food items over frequently to assure even cooking. You may need to rake hotter coals closer to your pot as you cook to ensure thorough cooking.
- You'll enjoy your meals more if you use what's local to make the recipes, especially if you've foraged for or caught it yourself.
- Try some of your favorite recipes over a campfire. Choose recipes that don't have a lot of steps and don't require a lot of bowls, pots, and pans. You'll be cooking like a pro in no time.
- All of the recipes in this book are just meant to get you started. Add your own variations to the meals. If you're

not a big sausage fan, use ground beef. If you didn't pack in Old Bay Seasoning, try your favorite blend. Check out the Simple Ingredient Substitutions table in Chapter 5 for more ideas.

- To get a sense of the possibilities, try cooking in a variety of ways—on the coals, in foil, using a Dutch oven, on a stick. You'll see that just about any recipe you can dream up at home can be made in camp.

— Chapter 17 —

PREPARING
UNCONVENTIONAL
FOODS

"He was a bold man who first ate an oyster."

—Jonathan Swift

If you find yourself in an unexpected situation where your pack is empty and you're still out in the wilderness, you don't have to rely only on the nuts and acorns you can glean from your surroundings. You can also forage for unconventional foods—things we don't normally think of as food.

But even in a non-emergency situation, you may want to learn to love grubs. Why eat bugs if we don't have to? Probably the number one reason to get used to eating bugs is that they are very healthy to eat. Most bugs, depending on species, are full of protein, fiber, healthy fats, vitamins, and essential minerals. Grasshoppers actually contain more protein pound for pound than ground beef. Grasshoppers also pick up flavor easily during cooking so if you don't like the flavor of your local species it is easy to change.

Bugs in general are one of the most prolific food sources on earth. This alone makes them worth understanding as a food source and trying something new is always interesting at the least. Dried bugs can easily be ground and mixed to extend existing resources like flour and other grains, and the risk of infectious disease is minimal at best compared to actual meat from animals. Most of us already consume bugs and their larva or eggs without realizing it in our foods anyway. This is just the next step and it has been a traditional dietary source in many countries since ancient times.

INSECTS YOU CAN EAT

Remember that most of the things you look for as bait for fishing are actually edible as well in an emergency. While you can eat most insects raw, they usually taste better cooked. Cooking helps kill any bacteria and makes the insects more appealing to eat.

To prepare, remove heads, wings, legs, and antennae to make the insects go down easier (this also helps eliminate potential sources of contamination).

- All worms like night crawlers and red worms are easy protein sources and very rich in proteins at that. To process a worm just start at one end and squeeze all the brown stuff out and you can consume it raw. Or you can soak them for several hours to get the dirt out. You can also use in stews and soups if you desire.
- Grasshoppers should be skewered and cooked well as they can carry tapeworms but are edible just the same. Pull the head off first (the insides should come out, too). Crickets and locusts can also be eaten roasted, fried, or boiled.

- Ants are small and take lots to make a meal but throwing them in a pot and melting some chocolate on them will make them go easier. You can also roast them and season them with salt. Carpenter ants, leaf-cutter ants, and honeypot ants are all fair game.
- Bees and wasps can be roasted and their larvae fried in butter. Remove stingers first.
- If you can find a termite mound run a stick into the mound and wait for it to fill with termites, then consume them raw. It may not be pleasant but it is food. (You can use this same technique to catch ants—find an anthill and run a stick into it.)
- Grubs are also fairly high in protein and can be roasted in hot embers and eaten if needed. When consuming large grubs raw it is a good idea to remove the head with a sharp knife to avoid the mandibles.
- Snails and slugs can carry parasites, so it's best to cook them before eating.
- Scorpions are not bad. Cut the poison sack off the end of the tail connected to the stinger and cook on coals or eat raw if needed.

INSECTS YOU SHOULDN'T EAT

Some insects are poisonous or may be likely to be contaminated in some way. Avoid eating these insects:

- Caterpillars should be left alone as some are poisonous.
- I steer clear of most arachnids (eight-legged critters). This is my own preference, of course, but if I cannot positively identify the source of food I do not eat it, so my recommendation is stay with common insects we all know from

childhood. As with caterpillars, some arachnids are poisonous, so be careful if you choose to consume these.

- Centipedes and millipedes are generally off the menu for me as well because of identification concerns—millipedes are poisonous and centipedes aren't, but it can be hard to tell them apart.
- Brightly colored insects (yellow, orange, green) should be avoided as they are generally poisonous. Stick with black and brown.
- Don't eat insects with strong odors. They may be poisonous or diseased.
- Don't eat disease-carrying insects such as mosquitoes and ticks.

TIPS AND TRICKS

- Catching insects can be a challenge for people used to shooing them away. One simple method is to dig a hole in the dirt near where you've seen insects such as crickets, and place a jar or container inside. In the container, place a piece of leftover food. In a few hours, you should have collected some bugs. Put the lid on the container and you have the makings for lunch.
- Grubs and other bugs like to live on the underside of logs; turn over enough and you'll have a meal.
- Flying insects are attracted to light. You can catch them with a net.
- You can grind insects into a paste and season it, then eat like a dip.
- If you want to test out bug eating before your next camping trip, you can order mealworms and other insects online or purchase them at a local pet store (live insects are often used to feed reptiles).

— Chapter 18 —
FORAGING

"Let food be thy medicine and medicine be thy food."

—HIPPOCRATES

Trapping game, catching fish, and scrounging for grubs aren't your only options for finding food in the wild. You can also forage for nuts, berries, and other edible plants. Many of these food items also serve a medicinal purpose.

COMMON EDIBLE PLANTS

A lot of common plants that grow in many front yards are edible. Clover, dandelion, plantain, burdock, and violets are not uncommon in rural areas, and they are quite tasty. However, gaining an understanding of the multitude of wild edibles takes study and several reference guides at a minimum to make sure what we are consuming is what we think it is. We must be careful as some plants are highly toxic.

CHOOSING THE RIGHT PLANTS

A good rule of thumb taught by a popular forager know as Green Deane is to ITEMize plants.

- **I**dentification. Identify them positively with several sources. If you misidentify a plant and eat it, you may get sick.
- **T**ime of year. Are they growing in the proper time of year according to references? If a plant that you think is rhubarb (for example) looks ready to pick in September, you may have the wrong plant; in the Northern Hemisphere, rhubarb is harvested in early spring.
- **E**nvironment. Make sure they are growing in the proper environment. If a plant is supposed to like growing in dry areas and you find it in a wet, boggy spot, you may have the wrong plant.
- **M**ethods. Understand the proper methods of harvest and preparation before consuming. In some cases you can eat the leaves but not the stem, or vice versa. Sometimes the berries are poisonous but the foliage is not, or vice versa. Some plants can be eaten raw but others must be cooked before consuming.

Spend time with someone else who has this knowledge as you are learning.

WILD EDIBLES

Here are some common plants that can be valuable resources in the wild:

- **Cattails** are nature's supermarket and pharmacy. The young shoots are edible raw or boiled; you can boil and eat the rootstock tubers as well. The pollen collected from the seed heads can be used as flour, and you can eat the young seed heads like corn on the cob.

- **Field parsnip** was used as a staple food for centuries but is now forgotten by most; the root of this plant is a great starch and can be baked like a potato. Warning: contact dermatitis can occur when handling this plant.
- **Dandelions** are a great green for a salad or can be eaten on the fly; they are full of vitamin A, and the flower tops are edible as well. Dandelion root is a good coffee substitute when dried and ground.
- Young leaves of the **burdock** plant are especially good for salad greens, and the large taproot is fine starch.
- **Arrowhead** is another water plant with an edible tuber that has high starch content.
- **Bulbs** can be stored in a cool, dry place for a whole season. Some great plants with edible bulbs include wild garlic or onion garlic. Ramps and leeks also contain edible and delicious bulbs.
- **Yellow nut grass** is another edible root plant native around areas of water where cattails and arrowhead are found.

WILD ONION AND WILD GARLIC SAUSAGE PATTIES

Use wild onion and wild garlic to spice up your sausage patties.

Finely mince fresh-picked wild onion and wild garlic. Mix into ground sausage and fry as normal in a pan over medium heat.

HERBS TO THE RESCUE

What if you're having a bit of tummy trouble but you don't have any Tums on hand? You know that coriander can help with digestive issues, but you didn't pack any in. What can you do? Sometimes the best herb is the herb you have! You may not always have the specific herb you want in a given situation so sometimes you just have to wing it. That is where understanding a bit more about herbal properties comes in to play.

Be as proactive with herbs as you are with other resources, like fire-building materials. Collect them as you go—especially if you haven't packed in something to care for an issue that may arise.

One thing I tell my students is to learn to positively identify the harmful plants first. There are far fewer of these, and then you know beyond that you are safe to consume or use what you find. What harmful plants you are likely to encounter depends on where you are, but some common ones are jimson weed (thorn apple), oleander, larkspur, and the twigs and foliage of wild cherries. The color insert in this section will help you identify some of these more common toxic plants.

BUSHCRAFT TIP

Charcoal isn't, of course, a plant, but I mention it here as it can be an indispensable resource in case of accidental food or plant poisoning. Ground in water, it will immediately induce vomiting and has absorbent qualities to remove leftover toxins from the stomach.

PLANT PROPERTIES

Once we have assured ourselves through proper education that a plant is safe to use and consume, we should begin to experiment and learn to not only identify the plant in all seasons but we should experiment with it as a tea, as a wash, as a poultice, and so on. We can research what the plant is good for. Remember that many plants act differently on different

people and getting to know what works well for you is important. To me it is very important to understand certain things
about a plant, since that gives me lots of clues as to its uses
beyond a food source.

MEDICINAL PROPERTIES OF PLANTS		
PLANT	USE	NOTES
Cattail	Tooth and gum care	Cattail has a very good gel that is present at the base of the sheath when the shoots are pulled out. This gel is anesthetic and antiseptic; you can liken it to aloe, as it is great for local pain relief from burns or stings. The young shoots of this plant make great toothbrushes as well.
Mullein	Cold/congestion, female cycle needs	Mullein has been used for centuries as a decongestant and is great for cough and cold remedies; the large, soft leaves of this plant can be used as wound dressings and are absorbent for female needs.
Jewelweed	Contact dermatitis	Jewelweed plant has chemicals within its juices that help alleviate the symptoms of contact dermatitis from poison ivy and other plants. The freshly picked plant can be rubbed on the skin. It is important to use this plant as soon as possible after contact from a problem plant.
Plantain	Bites/stings	Plantain can be used as a poultice by chewing the plant and then placing the macerated leaves on a sting or bite. It helps to draw out foreign objects such as splinters and thorns as well as the poison from a sting.

Mint	Headache	Mint has many excellent properties for general and medical use. Fresh mint leaves rubbed on the temples will help ease minor headaches. A decoction of mint can also be gargled for sore throats.
Mint and dandelion	Upset stomach	Dried mint and dandelion infusions are good for an upset stomach and will help relieve diarrhea.
Mint and yarrow	Cold and flu symptoms	An infusion or tea can be made with mint and yarrow to relieve cold and flu symptoms.
Yarrow	Blood coagulant/cold and flu care/insect repellent	Yarrow has been known throughout history for its abilities to clot blood from deep wounds; it also has anti-inflammatory properties. It will induce sweating when consumed as a tea and helps to break fevers. Recent studies have also shown that it's a great insect repellent.
Boneset	Deep bruises, breaks, fevers	Boneset as an infusion will help break a fever, while a poultice of the green leaves will help with deep bruises and even bone repair.

APPLICATION OF MEDICINAL PLANTS

Medicinal plants are mostly used in four ways:

1. **Poultice:** By gathering the plant leaves and flowers raw and macerating (crushing) them, you can form a poultice. This can then be steeped in boiled water or even chewed in the mouth (spit poultice) if it's an emergency, then placed directly on the affected area and wrapped with a bandanna or bandaging.

2. **Infusion tea:** To make a tea or an infusion, steep as you would a poultice for approximately 10–15 minutes, and then consume the liquid after straining.

3. **Decoction:** A decoction is much like an infusion but requires the material to be boiled, not steeped. This method is used for any bark material or roots. The liquid is then strained and consumed after boiling away half the liquid.

4. **Wash:** A wash is an infusion used to clean the affected area. In this case, the plant is not eaten at all.

USING YOUR SENSES

Tasting and feeling plants can give us lots of clues about their uses (once we are sure they are safe to eat). The sensations plants give us on the palate are very indicative of what they will do within our body as well. Generally to aid in an issue we look for plants that produce the opposite of existing conditions. So, for example, a hot or pungent herb will warm up the chills. A citrusy plant will cool down a warm body.

Put it in your mouth, chew it up, roll it around; feel what it is doing on the palate and how it tastes. Based on taste, you'll be able to divide it into one of four categories:

1. **Biters:** Plants that have a bitter or acrid taste are generally good medicine for colds and flu. They will generally be both antiseptic and antiviral in nature.

2. **Mucilaginous:** Plants that make the mouth water or are slimy will be good for constipation, as they will "grease the pipes," so to speak. They will be good for dry irritated sinuses, as well as burns.

3. **Astringents:** Plants that are astringent will pucker your mouth or dry out your palate and will do the same thing in

the body or on the skin. They will dry poison ivy, help dry up diarrhea, and cure a runny nose.

4. **Carminatives:** These plants will feel warming or spicy, and will be great for stomach upset and general relief of gas and discomfort in the digestive tract.

BUSHCRAFT TIP

Most wild herbs can be air-dried for later use. You can grind these dried herbs into flavorings for food and teas. A few of my favorites are mustard seed, garlic mustard, mint, shepherd's purse, and dock seeds.

NUTS

Rich in protein, nuts are some of the easiest plant-based food resources to harvest.

PINE NUTS

All pine nut seeds are edible so you do not need to worry about identifying different species. Some do, however, have larger seeds than others and, even though you can eat them green, the older ones taste better. The trick is to catch them just at the right time before they drop from the pinecones. Look for cones that are turning brown but have not yet opened. Arrange them around a fire and the warmth will force the cones open so that you can collect the seeds.

HICKORY NUTS

Hickory nuts are delicious and especially valuable because their shells efficiently lock out moisture and insects so they keep for a very long time. Most folks do not care to fool with hickory nuts because they can be so difficult to open. And after all that work, oftentimes you will end up with small pieces of shell everywhere and only a tiny bit of meat.

Let me share a secret with you. You have to take advantage of the internal structure of the hull itself to break it cleanly. I prefer to use an axe, but any hammering device—even just a stone—will work. Turn the nut so that it is lying sideways and the sharp, raised edge is on top. Basically, turn it to the spot where it wobbles and will not stand on its own. Then strike the seam in a spot about one-third of the way from the base of the stem. If you follow these steps, you should easily pop the nut into three pieces every time with plenty of exposed meat for the picking.

WALNUTS

Walnuts, specifically black walnuts, are a totally different animal from hickory nuts and must be treated differently. If possible, collect them before they fall from the tree and then store them until they turn black. If you do collect any from the ground, inspect them very closely for worm holes.

Remove the outer skins from the shells when they turn black and use the skins for dyes and medicines. Once you have revealed the nut shells themselves you can then break them open and eat the meat inside. Walnuts do not store in the shell as well as hickory nuts. If you decide to save them for future use, dry them before storing. Leave them in the shell and crack open just before eating.

FRUIT, VEGETABLES, AND HERBS

Fruit like raspberries, blackberries, and blueberries can be found in many parts of the country. Berries are energizing to eat and add vitamins and fiber to your diet.

FORAGING FOR BERRIES

Take extra care to make certain you can positively identify any berries before eating them. When in doubt, do not eat!

When looking for berries, scan the area from ground level to eye level. Look for low fruit trees and bushes. A lot of species are creepers so scan the ground very well. Remember that berry plants are biologically constructed to protect themselves from birds, so they are often hiding under greenery or surrounded with thorns. Keep a close eye out for poison ivy too.

FRUIT FORAGING

FRUIT	WHERE TO LOOK	SEASON
Blueberries	Blueberries grow in bush form. They flourish in acidic soil so you can sometimes find them in dried-up beaver ponds or near oak trees. They grow particularly well in sunny meadows.	Flowers in spring, berries in summer.
Elderberries	Moist forest soil along trails and around open fields.	Bloom June to July; fruits appear in late summer into fall.
Raspberries	Grow in bushes, usually found in areas that receive full sun.	Blossom in spring, fruit in summer.
Blackberries	Grow in small patches of brambly-looking vines. Look in areas near drainage ditches or trails.	Bloom in midsummer, eat in late summer.
Wild cherries	Grow rapidly from seeds dropped by birds so they are usually found as colonies of trees in clearings.	Blossoms in spring, fruits in summer; often hold until fall.
Cranberries	Grow best in acidic soil and bogs.	Ripen in the fall and usually stay a plant through the winter.
Strawberries	Grow close to the ground anywhere.	Blossom in spring; fruit in early summer.

Mulberries	Can be white, red, or black.	Very hardy, can survive in extremely cold temperatures.
Wild grapes	Occur throughout the eastern woodlands in several species.	Very hardy and cold-weather resistant.
Autumn olive	This species is invasive and grows in mostly field edges.	Blooms in early fall and becomes better after the first frost so it is a cold-weather plant.

BUSHCRAFT TIP

Many fruits and plants also produce natural dyes. Raspberry will make red, goldenrod is deep brown, pokeberries make a purple dye, bloodroot is orange to reddish. Dyes made from berries can be soaked in a hot fixative of salt water, while most plants will require a vinegar for fixing.

OTHER EDIBLE PLANTS

Many plants provide storable food resources such as seeds, seasonings, or bulbs. These food items can be processed and dried for later use.

BULBS

Bulbs can be stored in a cool, dry place for a whole season. There are some great plants with edible bulbs to be found in the woodlands, including wild garlic or onion garlic. This last is one of my favorites for sure. Ramps and leeks also contain edible and delicious bulbs.

ROOTS AND TUBERS

Cattail contains an edible starchy tuber that can be eaten as well as stored dry. Arrowhead is another water plant with an edible tuber that has high starch content. Burdock contains a large taproot similar to the potato and can be easily stored for later use if kept dry. Dandelion root makes a good drink or coffee substitute. You can even dry it and grind it down for later use in a hot drink. Yellow nut grass is another edible root plant native around areas of water where cattails and arrowhead are found.

TIPS AND TRICKS

- I discourage you from eating wild mushrooms at all since many are highly toxic.
- You don't have to learn about every wild plant in order to forage. Learn about the edibles in your area or where you like to camp. Local knowledge is what matters.
- You can find local experts at plant societies or through the extension service.
- Try a taste before you eat in bulk. Everyone is different. Plants that one person can eat and enjoy will make another sick.
- Regarding nuts, be careful of mildew, which is the real enemy of any seed. Keeping them dry is the key.
- Knowing some basic plant lore can keep you from wasting time. Nearly 100 percent of all white berries are toxic, for example; you don't need to bother finding out if the white-berried plant that grows in your local woods is edible. It probably isn't.

Chapter 19

PRESERVING CAUGHT AND FORAGED FOODS

"Good food is very often, even most often, simple food."
—ANTHONY BOURDAIN, *KITCHEN CONFIDENTIAL*

As you consider harvesting the resources from the world around you, you should consider what can be preserved. Letting food spoil or otherwise go unused isn't just wasteful, it creates more work for you.

Humans have been preserving food since the beginning of time, from cooking a large quantity of meat in order to make it last for a few days longer to burying it in snow to keep it fresh. There are a variety of ways to preserve meat and process plant food sources to extend their use.

FLOURS AND MEALS

Plant-based flours and meals can be used in many recipes and are a good way to preserve some plants.

ACORN FLOUR

Acorn flour was a staple food item for many Native peoples throughout history and remains a major source of food for forest animals today. I tend to seek out white oak acorns because they have fewer tannins and taste less bitter. Tannins within the acorn can give it a very astringent taste. It is important that acorns are processed correctly so they have a gentler flavor.

To process, you must first remove the shells. A rock or an axe can do this job efficiently. Then place the crushed acorns in a bowl of water where the shells will float and the meat will sink. Toss the shells. You want to process the meat down to the smallest size granules possible so you will want to leach the meat and remove the tannins.

To do this, drop the meat of the acorns in a clean batch of boiling water and let them cook until the water becomes brown. This discoloration is from the tannins. Place the acorn meat in another pot of boiling water and repeat the process. Make sure the water in the second pot is already boiling because if the acorns come in contact with cold water the process will undo itself. You will likely need to move the acorn meat to a new pot of boiling water 3–4 times before the staining stops. When the majority of the tannins have been removed, the water will start to run clean.

In an emergency, the acorns can be leached in running creek water by placing them in a cloth sack and leaving them in the creek for a week or so. Just know that the resulting flavor is not as reliable as what you get with the boiling method.

Once the meat is well soaked and clean you can grind it into a meal for hot cereal, use it as a bread ingredient, or dry it out and store it for later use. If you decide to save the acorn flour for later, plan to soak it in water before you use it to rehydrate it to its mushy status.

BUSHCRAFT TIP

The tannins that give acorns their astringent taste can be a great resource for other things such as medicines and tanning. Save the liquid from the first boiling pot of water you used to leech the acorn meat and reserve it for later use. Astringents work best for external use in a wash or poultice, but the solution will be antiparasitic as well.

CATTAIL FLOUR

Cattail makes the best form of starchy flour that nature has to offer, and the process of extracting it is not overly complicated. First you will need to collect a good bucketful of cattail roots. Loosen the soil around the cattail and its root area. Then put your hand at the base of the stalk and pull to release the entire plant with the root. At this point you can ditch the stalks and just hang on to the roots. Once you have washed them thoroughly and peeled them, place them in a bucket of clean water. Now begin to break up the roots, which causes the flour to separate from the fibers. Continue until you have separated all the fibers in the roots. As you work, the flour will settle at the bottom of the bucket. Pour out the excess water and dump the remaining mush on a flat surface where it can dry in the sun. Once the flour is completely dry, store it in a cool, dry place away from insects.

BUSHCRAFT TIP

The center of the cattail shoot is a nutrient-dense edible resource that makes an excellent vegetable you can simmer in soups or sauté as a side dish. Harvest the cattail shoots in dry weather so that the ground is not too muddy. Select large stalks that have not begun to flower, and separate the outer leaves from the core of the stalk. Discard these tough outer layers until you get down to the soft center. This process requires a lot of peeling, and your hands might get pretty sticky, but the product is delicious and rich in vitamins including vitamin C, beta-carotene, and potassium.

CATTAIL ACORN BREAD

2 cups acorn flour
2 cups cattail flour
2¼ teaspoons active dry yeast
1½ teaspoons salt
⅓ cup maple syrup
½ cup water
1 cup milk
2 tablespoons vegetable oil

You can mix these ingredients into a dough and throw it on some hot coals to make ash cakes.

ASH CAKES

Ash cakes are one of the easiest things to make in camp, and self-rising JAW mix works great for this. In the old farm days these were cooked on a farm hoe and called hoe cakes.

What I like to do is just mix in the bag, so I open it, pour in a few tablespoons of water, and stir to create a ball on the top of the other dry powder that did not absorb water. The ball should have the consistency of cookie dough. Take the ball out of the bag and sprinkle with some dry mix after flattening. Then place on hot coals, turning once during the cooking. It takes about 5–7 minutes to cook. Wipe off the ash after cooking. You can use this same formula for cooking on a shovel over coals.

SAPS

In the early winter months, many trees can be tapped for their sap but maples and birches are the best sources. This liquid makes a delicious drink straight from the tree on a cold morning or it can be further rendered into syrup by boiling it down to evaporate the water content.

MAPLE SYRUP

Maple syrup is made by further rendering the sap so that it becomes a sweet sticky liquid. Maple syrup can be used to sweeten any food or drink and keeps very well if stored properly. Once the sap is collected, pour it into a cooking pot until the pot is about ¾ full. Next boil the sap to evaporate all the water content. This will take several hours of constant boiling. The most difficult thing about making maple syrup is knowing exactly when the water has completely evaporated and the syrup itself has started to boil.

When this happens, the liquid will actually burn, something you want to avoid. Keep an eye on the color. The syrup should gradually turn gold and then darken until it becomes the mahogany shade of maple syrup. Once the syrup is complete you can strain the liquid to get rid of any particles that might have fallen into the concoction during the long boiling process. Pour into glass jars or plastic containers and store in a cool place. It should last in the refrigerator for about 6 months.

MAPLE SUGAR

Maple syrup can be even further processed into a delicious sweetener called maple sugar. Bring maple syrup to a boil and skim off the air bubbles as they rise. Reduce the heat a little if it starts to boil over the sides of the pot. When the air bubbles stop appearing, remove the liquid from the heat and transfer it to a wooden bowl. Stir for at least 5 minutes to remove any remaining moisture and then let it stand until it turns hard. This hard material can be ground into sugar and stored in a cool place.

MEAT

Preserving meat, no matter which method you choose, is a critical process because meat spoils very quickly, especially if you do not have access to refrigeration. Here are a few ways of preserving meat from your hunting or trapping campaign so that it can be safely consumed later.

SALT DRYING

Moisture is the enemy in meat preservation because it allows bacteria to grow. The process of drying meat involves pulling moisture from the meat at a slow rate so that the outside of the meat does not dry first. If the outside of the meat dries too quickly, moisture might get trapped inside, which will cause the meat to go rancid. With this understanding, two environmental conditions are necessary for properly drying meat:

1. A humidity level of about 30 percent or less
2. A few straight days with an even temperature where there is little fluctuation from day to night

For this reason, winter is generally not a good time to air-dry meat. Be careful in the spring that the weather is not too humid. Consider also the meat that will be used. Meats containing high concentrations of fat hold moisture, which makes the fat go rancid quickly.

If you do not have the means to cool the meat in a refrigerator, then you will need to salt it immediately after gutting the animal. All of the fatty tissue must be removed from the muscle meat before getting started. Then slice each piece of meat into long thin strips that are similar in size so that you can achieve even drying. Prepare a heavy salt solution into which each strip will be dipped before hanging.

SALT-DRIED MEAT AND FISH

*This solution will add flavor to the meat,
speed up the drying, and keep insects away.*

20 ounces salt
1 gallon water
Meat strips

To make a salt solution for drying meat and fish, stir salt into water until the salt is dissolved.

Dip the strips into the salt solution right before hanging. Suspend the meat strips vertically by the thickest end. Attach them to a line with loops of cordage of a small diameter if possible. Dried meat can then be stored in a breathable bag. You can eat it just as it is or rehydrate right before use.

SUN DRYING

Sun drying works best with fish, but the main concepts are the same regardless of the game you're sun drying. Again, evaporating the moisture from the inside layers to the outside is absolutely critical. Remove the heads and guts and then split the fish right at the spine. Now you should have two pieces, side by side with the skin on top of each. From here, cut the fish into several equal chucks. Fish will generally dry more quickly than red meat. Dip the strips into the salt solution. Dry the fish strips on racks, which you can easily fashion with two tripods and a cross-stick.

JERKY

You can make jerky by adding a good salt solution and some spice to the meat, which is then dried over a low-heat fire about 120°F. Cut the meat into lean, thin strips before drying.

Making jerky is different from salt drying because when making jerky, direct heat (not just the sun) is used to hasten the process. Hunters used this process long ago because it does not necessarily require salt or rubs (although those extras can give it a sensational taste) and it makes storage and transport easy. They would eat all they could at the kill site and then dry the rest, which substantially reduces the weight of the meat. If done properly, 1 pound of meat will reduce to about 4 ounces. When finished, the meat should crack when bent but not snap in half. It should be dry and not moist or greasy.

COLD SMOKING

The cold-smoking process is similar to making jerky in that you cut meat into thin strips, then salt and dry it with heat. Here, meat is dried at a temperature that is lower than what you use for jerky, about 85°F. You want a fire with lots of smoke to add flavor (and deter bugs). This method takes 12–24 hours in most cases.

COLD HANGING

In the winter, if the temperatures linger around freezing for a few days, meat can safely hang to dry. The cold temperatures ensure that bacteria do not develop. In this process, the meat does not need to be deboned and cut into strips but the animal must be completely gutted and opened with a cross-stick in the breast so that the carcass stays open while it dries.

TIPS AND TRICKS

- Meal planning can help cut down on the need to preserve foods you've gathered or trapped. But be flexible; it's easier to carry out the JAW packets that you packed in because you thought you might need them than it is to preserve all the trout you caught; eat the trout and save the JAW packets for next time.

- Remember to store all food in bear-safe containers.
- Except for when you're drying foods, keep them out of direct sunlight as this tends to speed the spoiling process.
- Whether you're at home or in the bush, the principles of food safety are always the same. Cold foods need to stay cold; hot foods need to stay hot. The range between 40°F and 140°F is known as the "danger zone" because this is where most food spoilage occurs (bacteria grows rapidly in this temperature range).
- Don't leave food out when you leave the campsite. It doesn't take long for squirrels, raccoons, and other animals to come investigate—and leave a mess.

PART 4

Emergency
Cooking

— Chapter 20 —
COOKING WITH YOUR ENGINE

"To succeed, planning alone is insufficient. One must improvise as well."

—Isaac Asimov

If you're caught in an emergency situation where your typical methods of cooking food aren't available, you can use one of several different unconventional methods of cooking. The first is to use your car.

The engine compartment of a running vehicle traps a ton of heat, and depending on what and how you are cooking there are a good range of temperatures that can be manipulated by raising and lowering the hood.

Remember that there are all sorts of fumes and possible contaminants under the hood, so anything cooked should be covered with a lid or wrapped in foil if possible. Shallow and wide pots and pans will heat faster than tall and narrow ones for any heat source but for this it will help even more.

The radiator is about 180–190°F while the car is running as long as the fan is working. The areas closer to the engine block such as the exhaust manifold will be hotter than this, so you have a range of heat levels. The best cooking like this is done either in the can with canned foods or in aluminum foil or foil tins. These are the safest methods and will not ruin a good container or contaminate the food. A small log or rock used as a wedge will let you rest the hood almost closed to keep the heat trapped but will also allow you to observe the goodness as your meal cooks.

BUSHCRAFT TIP

Anything you have left from the last meal can be wrapped into an aluminum-foil envelope and reheated near the manifold.

You can even place foil-wrapped meals in wire mesh and tie them down so they can be cooked while driving down the trail for a hot lunch at midday. Of course there is no exact science to cooking in an engine and there are many variables, but using precooked foods or heat-and-eat meals will work fairly well in most conditions.

ENGINE-COOKED RECIPES

CANNED SURPRISE

Wanna have some fun camping?

Remove the labels from 5–6 cans of random food from ravioli to beans-and-weenies, then make the kids pick a random can

Place the unidentified can near the manifold to cook about 20 minutes, then serve.

BUICK BURRITOS

Leftover cooked meat (a few ounces per tortilla)
Beans, cheese, salsa, hot sauce (as desired)
Corn tortillas

Wrap cooked meat and fixings into a corn tortilla. Wrap in foil and lay across the radiator lengthwise about 10–15 minutes. Serve.

BAKED STUFFED POTATOES

1 medium potato (russet works well for this)
Butter, bacon bits, chopped onion

Cut open the potato lengthwise. Add butter, bacon bits, and chopped onion. Wrap well in foil and place on manifold about 30–40 minutes until a fork will pass in and out easily.

CHEROKEE CHEESE BREAD

I use my Jeep for this now and again, hence the name.

Ready-mix garlic cheese biscuit mix
Water (as indicated on the package directions)

Stir water into biscuit mix and pour into a small loaf pan. Cover with heavy foil and bake near the manifold 12–15 minutes or until a fork comes out dry.

TIPS AND TRICKS

- As with anything, trying it at home before you have to resort to it in an emergency can help you be prepared for whatever happens.
- Almost any recipe that requires just oven cooking can be cooked on your engine. You will have to adjust cooking times.

- Always turn off the engine before putting food on the engine or taking it off.
- Only the metal parts of the engine will get hot enough to cook. You can gauge the relative heat of various parts of your engine by running the motor for a minute, then shutting it off, then quickly touching the various parts.
- Be sure any food you're cooking isn't blocking air flow, a moving part, or otherwise interferes with the proper working of the engine.

— Chapter 21 —

UNCONVENTIONAL FUELS AND FUEL TABS

"No one is born a great cook. One learns by doing."

—Julia Child

We are used to using a few common cooking fuels when camping. Wood and campfires are the simplest and most romantic. Propane and multi-fuel camp stoves like those made by Coleman are also common. In these days of ultra-light backpacking and hiking, alcohol-type stoves have also become quite popular, as well as smaller single-burner multi-fuel canister stoves.

When we look at unconventional fuels we are looking to what we can use if we are without all these items and cannot for some reason burn wood logs. Obviously anything flammable from gasoline to rubber will burn, but from a health and safety standpoint these are dangerous fuels for cooking. However, all common cooking oils will also burn and can be contained and used with a wick or multiple wicks to create a makeshift cooking surface.

BUSHCRAFT TIP

Candles will heat food well enough in an emergency. The more candles you use, the more candle power you have. Four of the 12-hour beeswax candles work pretty well.

WOOD CHIP BRICKS

Another easy thing you can do in camp is to mix wood shavings and beeswax for emergency cook fuels. To do this, pack any wood shaving (such as from a chainsaw or wood shop) into a small tin like a cat food can. Pour melted beeswax over the top and let dry. You now have a block of fuel that, if left in the can, will burn for a few hours if needed and get food plenty hot as well.

ANIMAL FAT

Animal fats will burn similarly to lard (which is actually a domestic animal fat rendered for cooking). To render tallow or deer fat, place the scraped fat from the animal in a pan on low heat until liquid forms. Use this as a fuel immediately or after cooling (when it has hardened and is set). It can also be used to replace cooking oil to grease a pan.

PINE SAP

Pine sap is a natural fuel that appears on pines anywhere they are injured. This sap can be collected and will burn very hot for a good long time depending on the amount you have collected. You can burn it in a metal container to contain the fuel source or place it directly on the ground and light it.

This resin will leave a sticky residue on any container placed above it for cooking, and you should never cook food without a container over this fuel as it will impart a bad taste on the food.

FUEL TABS AND SOLID FUELS

Solid fuels can be easier to transport than liquid fuels. Fuel tabs are solid fuels sold in tab form. They have several advantages over liquid fuels; they burn smokelessly, they don't leave ashes behind, and they can burn hotter. There are many sources for solid fuel tabs. Nowadays we can (and should) avoid the older-style surplus tabs, many of which were toxic in some form or another. Now we can get tabs that are much safer and do a pretty good job of cooking food in an emergency.

There are many brands available, and most use the same technology, but you can also save a bit of money and use the Weber charcoal grill starter blocks found in most lumberyards and home-and-garden stores during the grilling season.

The main thing to remember with artificial heat sources and solid fuels is food containment is important to taste as well as, sometimes, your health. Therefore, always cook in a pot (or with the food wrapped in foil) over these fuel sources instead of placing the food directly on the flames.

Foods that can cook at lower temperatures for shorter times are good choices for these types of alternative fuels. For example, just-add-hot-water meals will work better than stews, which require hours of cooking. Warming precooked meals will be easier and faster than cooking from raw.

TIPS AND TRICKS

- The Esbit tabs are about my favorite of the solid fuel tabs. They come individually packaged, are waterproof, and will boil 8 ounces of water in about 4 minutes.
- Tightly rolled newsprint saturated with melted wax is also an excellent fuel source that can be used for cooking when needed if made ahead of time.
- Do not cook open foods like meat on any artificial logs such as Duraflames, as these will taint the food. It is okay, however, to cook in pots, using the logs as a heat source.
- One good use of unconventional fuels is to use them to start a conventional fire. If you don't have any char to start a fire but you do have a fuel tab, you'll be eating dinner in no time.
- You can forego the need for an outside fuel source entirely and just pack in self-heating food! Each meal contains its own heating unit and is ready to eat in about 20 minutes.

— Chapter 22 —

MAKING A STOVE

"To me, unconventional thinking is approaching a problem and asking, 'Why not? Why can't something be done?' If someone can't give me a good reason why you can't do something, I find a way to do it."

—Eli Broad

Some of the best emergency stoves are made with natural materials that you may find around you. For example, a rocket stove can be made with a single log.

MAKING A ROCKET STOVE

A rocket stove is basically a portable stove you can build that will burn small-diameter wood and create a nice hot fire (hotter than a typical campfire). Fuel is burned in a chimney that directs the flames to the cooking surface.

The secret to the rocket stove is to create draw when air is lifted from below the fire up through the food on the cooking surface. A rocket stove can be built below ground, above ground, or made portable.

All rocket stoves require three components:

- Draft vent
- Feed tray
- Chimney

You can create the stove with pipe, cans, rocks, cinderblocks, bricks, or any other material that can be stacked. It can also be created from a single log with 2 holes bored into L fashion. See Figure 22.1.

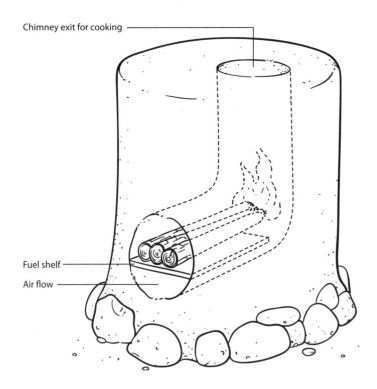

Chimney exit for cooking

Fuel shelf

Air flow

Figure 22.1 Rocket stove

SWEDISH FIRE TORCH

The Swedish fire torch is quick to make for a single use and very effective. Start with a bucked hardwood log that is fairly dry, about 10–12" diameter. Using an axe and mallet or a wedge, split the log into quarters. Place the quarters standing in a ring. Build a small fire in the center. This will work in a similar manner to the rocket stove, but the inner dry log will burn and you can place pots or pans on top for cooking. See Figure 22.2.

Figure 22.2 Swedish fire torch

CAN LAMP STOVE

To make a can lamp stove using a #10 can (this is a large can that can hold about a gallon), cut the can down till it's about 4" in height. Fill it with cooking oil or lard to about 3". Take some wire and create stands for multiple wicks of natural material. (Inner bark cordage will work in an emergency.) Four wicks should be enough. Place them in the bottom of the can. Let them absorb oil and then light them. Add a couple small ½"-diameter sticks on the outer edge to create air space and place the cook pot on the top. This method will not be as fast as many fuels but will work in an emergency. See Figure 22.3.

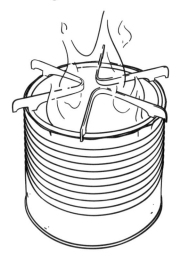

Figure 22.3

Can lamp stove

DOUBLE CAN STOVES

These stoves can be made from 2 cans with few supplies. Not all aluminum cans are created equal. The cans should be free of dents or dings when you start; the heavier the material the better. The advantage to a stove like this is the flame can be controlled if you have made a simmer ring (heat diffuser). The fuel it will burn comes in many forms, even grain alcohols, and it is very lightweight to carry.

1. Poke holes along the bottom edge of one opened can. About 12–16 holes will do the trick.

2. Cut out the bottom of this can. (At this point, the top and bottom of the can should have been removed.)
3. Cut the can down to about ¾" in height. This is the stove top.
4. Snip the edges of the stove top to form several tabs.
5. Cut the second can down to about 1" in height. This is the stove bottom.
6. Cut an inner wall from the leftover can material. Do this by cutting a strip about 1⅓" wide.
7. Notch the ends of the inner wall, cutting halfway through the strip from the top on one side and halfway through the strip from the bottom on the other. Then the ends will hook together and fit inside the stove bottom.
8. Cut 3 notches, evenly spaced, around one edge of the inner wall strip. Place the inner wall, notches down, inside the stove bottom. Place the stove top on, bending the tabs slightly so they fit inside the stove bottom.
9. For a permanent bond, use a high-temperature tape to keep the top and the bottom securely connected.
10. Create a pot stand to hold the cook pot over the flames. A piece of wire mesh placed over a ring of metal will serve.

To use the stove, pour denatured alcohol into the stove. Filling it about halfway will give you a burning time of about 10 minutes. Then light the fuel. The flame will be difficult to see, so listen carefully to hear it ignite. If the tape catches fire, don't worry. Just let the fuel burn off. See Figure 22.4.

Figure 22.4
Double can stove

TIPS AND TRICKS

- In an emergency, you can make a stove out of just about anything! The key is to understand what a fire needs (heat, oxygen, and fuel) and to identify items in the environment that can serve these purposes.
- Stoves can sometimes be used where campfires are prohibited, so they make a handy alternative.
- Remember, never cook on a camp stove indoors (inside a cabin, inside a tent). Always go outside to cook.
- On windy days, building a shield with aluminum foil can help keep your flame from flickering out.
- Never leave a camp stove unattended.

— Chapter 23 —
SOLAR
COOKING

"People who love to eat are always the best people."
—Julia Child

Solar cooking takes advantage of the sun's rays, a renewable resource, to cook, heat, or pasteurize food and drinks. The technique of this cooking is to concentrate heat by reflecting the radiant heat to a central location. It is different from drying, as cooking needs concentrated heat.

Solar cooking is a great way to cook food without leaving any environmental impact or when fire restrictions are in place.

There are many solar cookers on the market. Some are very expensive, some are less so, but you can improvise them in many ways. One of the easiest ways is to use a simple windshield reflector (the kind for your car, sold commonly in stores for about $5–$10). It also helps if the cooking container you are using is black for maximum absorption of heat. You can accomplish this with high-temperature black grill paint if needed.

WINDSHIELD REFLECTOR COOKER

Materials needed:

- A windshield reflector (one that folds like an accordion)
- 3 strips of hook-and-loop fastener (Velcro), about 1½" long each
- 5-gallon plastic bucket
- Black cook pot
- Cake rack (or wire frame or grill)
- Plastic baking bag

1. Separate the Velcro strips into the hook sides and the loop sides.
2. Spread the reflector out. One long end should have a section cut out for the rearview mirror.
3. Along the left side of that cutout, evenly place the hook sides of all 3 hook-and-loop strips and sew them down.
4. Do the same on the underside of the right side of the cutout, using the loop sides of the hook-and-loop strips.
5. When you're done, you should be able to bring the reflector sides together in the shape of a funnel, using the hook-and-loop fasteners to secure the reflector into this position.
6. Set the reflector in the plastic bucket.
7. Place the cook pot (with food to be cooked) on the cake rack, then place both inside the plastic baking bag. Set the rack and pot into the funnel so the rack rests on top of the bucket.
8. Tilt the reflector in the direction of the sun. After cooking, the oven can easily be disassembled and stored.

TIMING AND SOLAR COOKING

Everything takes longer to cook using a solar stove, but most things just get more tender the longer they cook, so times are flexible. For example, cut-up pieces of chicken take about 2 hours to cook but can be cooked for 4 hours without harming the taste. This means you can start a meal before leaving camp, then return hours later without worrying about your meal burning or overcooking.

BUSHCRAFT TIP

Make a baked potato just by adding clean potatoes to a dark, covered pot (no water needed). Don't add water to vegetables when using a solar cooker. Most vegetables (such as asparagus, cabbage, corn on the cob) will take 1½–2 hours to cook. Root vegetables like potatoes and carrots will take about 3 hours.

Most food takes about 3 times longer to cook in a solar oven than in a conventional oven. With experimentation, you'll be able to find the best times for your food. Remember that the brightness of the day will make a difference in how long it takes to cook a meal.

TIPS AND TRICKS

- Usually you will achieve best results if you cook foods in containers that are black.
- Using a glass lid on a pot can help concentrate the sun's power—but while durable, glass lids can break under tough camping conditions, so consider the pros and cons.
- You can even make bread, cakes, and cookies in a solar cooker. Give it a try.
- You may have to refocus the cooker on overcast days or when you're cooking a lot of food at once. Large quantities of food will cook more evenly if divided between several pots.
- Roasts, stews, and casseroles are great choices for solar cookery. Most recipes need less water when cooked in a solar cooker.

Appendix A

NUTRITIONAL VALUES OF GAME ANIMALS AND NUTS

The following tables give nutritional information for various game animals and nuts you may forage. Nutrition information assumes game animals have been roasted or stewed without added ingredients and that nuts are eaten raw.

GAME ANIMALS

FRESHWATER BASS, 3 OUNCES
Calories: 124 calories
Fat: 4 grams
Protein: 20.5 grams
Sodium: 76.5 mg
Carbohydrates: 0 grams
Sugars: 0 grams
Fiber: 0 grams

BEAVER, 3 OUNCES
Calories: 180 calories
Fat: 6 grams
Protein: 30 grams
Sodium: 50 mg
Carbohydrates: 0 grams
Sugars: 0 grams
Fiber: 0 grams

WILD BOAR, 3 OUNCES
Calories: 136 calories
Fat: 4 grams
Protein: 24 grams
Sodium: 51 mg
Carbohydrates: 0 grams
Sugars: 0 grams
Fiber: 0 grams

CARP, 3 OUNCES
Calories: 138 calories
Fat: 6 grams
Protein: 19 grams
Sodium: 53.5 mg
Carbohydrates: 0 grams
Sugars: 0 grams
Fiber: 0 grams

CHANNEL CATFISH, 3 OUNCES
Calories: 89 calories
Fat: 2 grams
Protein: 16 grams
Sodium: 42 mg
Carbohydrates: 0 grams

Sugars: 0 grams
Fiber: 0 grams

CLAMS, 1 CUP WITH LIQUID
Calories: 168 calories
Fat: 2 grams
Protein: 29 grams
Sodium: 127 mg
Carbohydrates: 6 grams
Sugars: 0 grams
Fiber: 0 grams

CRAYFISH, 3 OUNCES
Calories: 70 calories
Fat: 1 gram
Protein: 14 grams
Sodium: 80 mg
Carbohydrates: 0 grams
Sugars: 0 grams
Fiber: 0 grams

DEER, 3 OUNCES
Calories: 159 calories
Fat: 7 grams
Protein: 22 grams
Sodium: 66 mg
Carbohydrates: 0 grams
Sugars: 0 grams
Fiber: 0 grams

FROG LEGS, 1 OUNCE
Calories: 21 calories
Fat: 0 grams
Protein: 5 grams
Sodium: 16 mg
Carbohydrates: 0 grams
Sugars: 0 grams
Fiber: 0 grams

MUSKRAT, 3 OUNCES
Calories: 199 calories
Fat: 10 grams
Protein: 26 grams
Sodium: 103 mg
Carbohydrates: 0 grams

Sugars: 0 grams
Fiber: 0 grams

NORTHERN PIKE, 3 OUNCES
Calories: 96 calories
Fat: 1 gram
Protein: 21 grams
Sodium: 42 mg
Carbohydrates: 0 grams
Sugars: 0 grams
Fiber: 0 grams

OPOSSUM, 3 OUNCES
Calories: 188 calories
Fat: 9 grams
Protein: 26 grams
Sodium: 49 mg
Carbohydrates: 0 grams
Sugars: 0 grams
Fiber: 0 grams

RABBIT, 3 OUNCES
Calories: 147 calories
Fat: 3 grams
Protein: 28 grams
Sodium: 38 mg
Carbohydrates: 0 grams
Sugars: 0 grams
Fiber: 0 grams

RACCOON, 3 OUNCES
Calories: 217 calories
Fat: 12 grams
Protein: 25 grams
Sodium: 67 mg
Carbohydrates: 0 grams
Sugars: 0 grams
Fiber: 0 grams

SQUIRREL, 3 OUNCES
Calories: 147 calories
Fat: 4 grams
Protein: 26 grams
Sodium: 101 mg
Carbohydrates: 0 grams

Sugars: 0 grams
Fiber: 0 grams

TROUT, 3 OUNCES
Calories: 128 calories
Fat: 5 grams
Protein: 19 grams
Sodium: 48 mg
Carbohydrates: 0 grams
Sugars: 0 grams
Fiber: 0 grams

NUTS

ALMONDS, 1 OUNCE
Calories: 163 calories
Fat: 14 grams
Protein: 6 grams
Sodium: 0 mg
Carbohydrates: 6 grams
Sugars: 1 gram
Fiber: 3.5 grams

BRAZIL NUTS, 1 OUNCE
Calories: 186 calories
Fat: 19 grams
Protein: 4 grams
Sodium: 1 mg
Carbohydrates: 3.5 grams
Sugars: 1 gram
Fiber: 2 grams

CASHEWS, 1 OUNCE
Calories: 157 calories
Fat: 12 grams
Protein: 5 grams
Sodium: 3 mg
Carbohydrates: 9 grams
Sugars: 2 grams
Fiber: 1 gram

HAZELNUTS, 1 OUNCE
Calories: 179 calories
Fat: 18 grams
Protein: 4 grams
Sodium: 0 mg
Carbohydrates: 5 grams
Sugars: 1 gram
Fiber: 3 grams

MACADAMIA NUTS, 1 OUNCE
Calories: 204 calories
Fat: 22 grams
Protein: 2 grams
Sodium: 1 mg
Carbohydrates: 4 grams
Sugars: 1 gram
Fiber: 2 grams

PEANUTS, 1 OUNCE
Calories: 161 calories
Fat: 14 grams
Protein: 7 grams
Sodium: 5 mg
Carbohydrates: 5 grams
Sugars: 1 gram
Fiber: 2 grams

PECANS, 1 OUNCE
Calories: 196 calories
Fat: 20 grams
Protein: 3 grams
Sodium: 0 mg
Carbohydrates: 4 grams
Sugars: 1 gram
Fiber: 3 grams

PINE NUTS, 1 OUNCE
Calories: 191 calories
Fat: 19 grams
Protein: 4 grams
Sodium: 1 mg
Carbohydrates: 4 grams
Sugars: 1 gram
Fiber: 1 gram

PISTACHIOS, 1 OUNCE
Calories: 159 calories
Fat: 6 grams
Protein: 6 grams
Sodium: 0 mg
Carbohydrates: 8 grams
Sugars: 2 grams
Fiber: 3 grams

WALNUTS, 1 OUNCE
Calories: 175 calories
Fat: 17 grams
Protein: 7 grams
Sodium: 1 mg
Carbohydrates: 4 grams
Sugars: 1 gram
Fiber: 2 grams

GENERAL INDEX

INDEX OF RECIPES